Pre-GED Connection™

WITHDRAWN
WITHDRAWN

Social Studies

by Marion Castellucci, Elizabeth Kaplan, and Patricia McCormick

LiteracyLink® is a joint project of PBS, Kentucky Educational Television, the National Center on Adult Literacy, and the Kentucky Department of Education.

This project is funded in whole, or in part, by the Star Schools Program of the USDE under contract #R203D60001.

 **PBS** LiteracyLink®

 KET

 NCAL

Acknowledgments

LiteracyLink® Advisory Board

Lynn Allen, Idaho Public Television

Anthony Buttino, WNED-TV

Anthony Carnevale, Educational
    Testing Service

Andy Chaves, Marriott International, Inc.

Patricia Edwards, Michigan State University

Phyllis Eisen, Center for Workforce Success National
    Association of Manufacturers

Maggi Gaines, Baltimore Reads, Inc.

Marshall Goldberg, Association of Joint Labor
    Management Educational Programs

Milton Goldberg, National Alliance
    for Business

Neal Johnson, Association of Governing Boards of
    Universities and Colleges

Cynthia Johnston, Central Piedmont Community
    College

Sandra Kestner, Kentucky Department for Adult
    Education and Literacy

Thomas Kinney, American Association of Adult and
    Continuing Education

Dale Lipschultz, American Library Association

Lennox McLendon, National Adult Education
    Professional Development Consortium

Cam Messina, KLRN

Patricia Miller, KNPB

Cathy Powers, WLRN

Ray Ramirez, U.S. Department of Education

Emma Rhodes, (retired) Arkansas Department of
    Education

Cynthia Ruiz, KCET

Tony Sarmiento, Worker Centered Learning,
    Working for America Institute

Steve Steurer, Correctional
    Education Association

LaShell Stevens-Staley, Iowa PTV

Fran Tracy-Mumford, Delaware Department of
    Adult/Community Education

Terilyn Turner, Community Education,
    St. Paul Public Schools

**LiteracyLink®
Ex Officio Advisory Board**

Joan Auchter, GED Testing Service

Barbara Derwart, U.S. Department of Labor

Cheryl Garnette, OERI, U.S.
    Department of Education

Andrew Hartman, National Institute
    for Literacy

Mary Lovell, OVAE, U.S. Department
    of Education

Ronald Pugsley, OVAE, U.S. Department
    of Education

Linda Roberts, U.S. Department of Education

Joe Wilkes, OERI, U.S. Department of Education

LiteracyLink® Partners

LiteracyLink® is a joint project of:
    Public Broadcasting Service,
    Kentucky Educational Television,
    National Center on Adult Literacy, and the
    Kentucky Department of Education.

**Content Design and Workbook
Editorial Development**
    Learning Unlimited, Oak Park, Illinois

Design and Layout
    By Design, Lexington, Kentucky

Project Coordinators
    Milli Fazey, KET, Lexington, Kentucky
    Margaret Norman, KET, Lexington, Kentucky

Photo Credits

p. 50 Chuck Fishman-Woodfin Camp

p. 57 Peter Turnley/ CORBIS

p. 108 Peter Essick/ Aurora

This project is funded in whole, or in part, by the
Star Schools Program of the USDE under contract
#R203D60001.

PBS LiteracyLink® is a registered mark of the
Public Broadcasting Service.

Contents

Introduction

Welcome to *Pre-GED Social Studies*. This workbook is part of the *LiteracyLink®* multimedia educational system for adult learners and educators. The system includes *Pre-GED Connection*, which is used to build a foundation for GED-level study and *GED Connection*, which learners use to study for the GED Tests. *LiteracyLink* also includes *Workplace Essential Skills*, which targets upgrading the knowledge and skills needed to succeed in the world of work.

Pre-GED CONNECTION
consists of these educational tools:

26 VIDEO PROGRAMS shown on public television and in adult learning centers

ONLINE MATERIALS available on the Internet at http://www.pbs.org/literacy

FIVE Pre-GED COMPANION WORKBOOKS

Language Arts, Writing
Language Arts, Reading
Social Studies
Science
Mathematics

Instructional Programs

Pre-GED Connection consists of 26 instructional video programs and five companion workbooks. Each *Pre-GED Connection* workbook lesson accompanies a video program. For example, the first lesson in this book is *Program 11— Themes in U.S. History*. This workbook lesson should be used with *Pre-GED Connection Video Program 11— Themes in U.S. History*.

Who's Responsible for LiteracyLink®?

LiteracyLink was developed through a five-year grant by the U.S. Department of Education. The following partners have contributed to the development of the *LiteracyLink* system:

| PBS Adult Learning Service | Kentucky Educational Television (KET) | The National Center on Adult Literacy (NCAL) of the University of Pennsylvania | The Kentucky Department of Education |

All of the *LiteracyLink* partners wish you the very best in meeting all of your educational goals.

Before you start using the workbook, take some time to preview its features.

1. Take the **Pretest** starting on page 6. This will help you decide which areas you need to focus on. You should use the evaluation chart on page 17 to develop your study plan.

2. Work through the **workbook lessons**—each one corresponds to a video program.

   The *Before You Watch* feature sets up the video program:
   - **Think About the Topic** gives a brief overview of the video
   - **Prepare to Watch the Video** is a short activity with instant feedback that shows how everyday knowledge can help you better understand the topic
   - **Lesson Goals** highlight the main ideas of each video and workbook lesson
   - **Terms** introduces key reading vocabulary

   The *After You Watch* feature helps you evaluate what you have just seen in the program:
   - **Think About the Program** presents questions that focus on key points from the video
   - **Make the Connection** applies what you have learned to real-life situations

   Three *Social Studies Skills* sections correspond to key concepts in the video program.

   The **Thinking Skill** sections prepare you for the types of critical-thinking questions that you will see on the GED.

   The **Graphic Skill** sections introduce you to the charts, timelines, graphs, editorial cartoons, and maps that you will see on the GED.

   GED Practice allows you to practice with the types of questions that you will see on the actual test.

3. Take the **Posttest** starting on page 118 to determine your progress and whether you are ready for GED-level work.

4. Use the **Answer Key** to check your answers.

5. Refer to the **Social Studies Resources** at the back of the book, as needed.

For Teachers

Portions of *LiteracyLink* have been developed for adult educators and service providers. Teachers can use Pre-GED lesson plans in the ***LiteracyLink Teacher's Guide*** binder. This binder also contains lesson plans for ***GED Connection*** and ***Workplace Essential Skills***.

Social Studies Pretest

The Social Studies Pretest on the following pages is similar to the GED Social Studies Test. However, it has only 25 items, compared with 50 items on a regular GED Social Studies Test.

This Pretest consists of short passages, timelines, charts, maps, graphs, and other graphics about Social Studies. Each passage or graphic is followed by one or more multiple-choice questions. Read each passage, study the graphics, and then answer the questions. You may refer back to the passage or graphic whenever you wish.

The purpose of the Pretest is to evaluate your Social Studies knowledge and thinking skills. Do not worry if you cannot answer every question or if you get some questions wrong. The Pretest will help you identify the content areas and skills that you need to work on.

Directions

1. Read the sample passage and test item on page 7 to become familiar with the test format.

2. Take the test on pages 8 through 15. Read each passage, study the graphics, if any, and then choose the best answer to each question.

3. Record your answers on the answer sheet below, using a No. 2 pencil.

4. Check your work against the Answers and Explanations on page 16.

5. Enter your scores in the evaluation charts on page 17.

SOCIAL STUDIES PRETEST ANSWER SHEET

Name _____   Date _____

Class _____

1. ①②③④⑤	6. ①②③④⑤	11. ①②③④⑤	16. ①②③④⑤	21. ①②③④⑤
2. ①②③④⑤	7. ①②③④⑤	12. ①②③④⑤	17. ①②③④⑤	22. ①②③④⑤
3. ①②③④⑤	8. ①②③④⑤	13. ①②③④⑤	18. ①②③④⑤	23. ①②③④⑤
4. ①②③④⑤	9. ①②③④⑤	14. ①②③④⑤	19. ①②③④⑤	24. ①②③④⑤
5. ①②③④⑤	10. ①②③④⑤	15. ①②③④⑤	20. ①②③④⑤	25. ①②③④⑤

Sample Passage and Test Item

The following passage and test item are similar to those you will find on the Social Studies Pretest. Read the passage and the test item. Then go over the answer sheet sample and explanation of why the correct answer is correct.

Question 0 refers to the following passage.

The Eighteenth Amendment to the U.S. Constitution, passed in 1919, prohibited the manufacture, sale, and transportation of alcoholic beverages. In the first few years after the Prohibition amendment was passed, the law seemed to be a big success. Arrests for drunkenness and alcohol-related deaths declined. But gradually, more liquor was smuggled into the country or manufactured in illegal stills. Liquor again became widely available. Neither federal nor local governments were able to hire adequate staff to enforce the law. In fact, in big cities, the law was largely ignored.

When it became clear that Prohibition could not be enforced, Congress passed the Twenty-first Amendment, in 1933. That amendment repealed the Eighteenth Amendment, making alcoholic beverages legal again.

0. Why was the Eighteenth Amendment repealed?
    (1) It was illegal.
    (2) It was not enforceable.
    (3) Illegal liquor was being manufactured.
    (4) Smugglers were importing liquor from abroad.
    (5) There was a decline in alcohol-related deaths.

Marking the Answer Sheet

0. ① ② ③ ④ ⑤

The correct answer is **(2) It was not enforceable.** Therefore, answer space 2 is marked on the answer sheet, as shown above. The space should be filled in completely using a No. 2 pencil. If you change your mind about an answer, erase it completely.

Answer and Explanation

(2) It was not enforceable. (Comprehension) According to the passage, there were not enough law enforcement officials to prevent the manufacture, sale, and transportation of alcoholic beverages. Also, the law was openly being broken in large cities. Therefore, Congress concluded that the prohibition was not enforceable and repealed the Eighteenth Amendment.

Social Studies Pretest

Choose the <u>one best answer</u> to the questions below.

<u>Questions 1 and 2</u> refer to the following passage.

In colonial America, about 1.5 percent of births resulted in the death of the mother. Since typical mothers gave birth 5 to 8 times over the course of their lives, the chance of eventually dying in childbirth was about 1 in 8 for women during the 1600s and 1700s.

Women gave birth at home, assisted by female relatives and neighbors. If they were lucky, they also had an experienced midwife who was skilled in a variety of techniques to assist women in labor. Expert midwives were valued so much that some communities tried to attract them by offering salaries and rent-free houses. Still, colonial women referred to childbirth as "the greatest of earthly miseries" and "that evil hour I look forward to with dread."

1. In colonial America, what was a mother's chance of dying in childbirth?
    (1) about 1 in 100
    (2) about 1 in 50
    (3) about 1 in 25
    (4) about 1 in 8
    (5) about 1 in 2

2. Which of the following was the main reason a good midwife was valued in colonial communities?
    (1) She came from the upper classes.
    (2) She lived in a rent-free house.
    (3) She drew a salary from the community.
    (4) She freed relatives and friends of the duty of assisting in childbirth.
    (5) She improved women's chances of surviving childbirth.

3. After World War II, the Soviet Union's influence extended into Eastern Europe, which became communist. A communist government also came to power in the world's most populous nation—China. To prevent communism from spreading further, the United States developed the policy of containment. Under this policy, the United States tried to contain communism by being politically, economically, and militarily active.

    Which of the following is an example of the containment policy in action?
    (1) the threats President Truman made to draft workers who went on strike
    (2) the building of the interstate highway system, which linked U.S. cities
    (3) the Vietnam War, in which the United States supported South Vietnam against communist North Vietnam
    (4) the Iran hostage crisis, in which 52 Americans were held hostage in Tehran for more than a year
    (5) the accident at the Chernobyl nuclear plant in the Soviet Union, which spread harmful radiation throughout Europe

4. In the late 1800s companies would try to eliminate their competitors. If they could not do so, they would band together in a group called a trust. Trusts eliminated competition and enabled the companies to fix prices. Antitrust laws, beginning with the Sherman Antitrust Act of 1890, restricted trusts.

    What did the government value more than business profits in this situation?
    (1) competition   **(4)** negativity
    (2) innovation   **(5)** democracy
    (3) honor

1860	1861	1862	1863	1864	1865
• Lincoln elected 16th president • South Carolina secedes from the Union	• Six more Southern states secede; Confederacy formed • Confederacy attacks Fort Sumter • Lincoln declares war • Four more Southern states join the Confederacy • Confederacy wins battle at Bull Run	• Union forces capture South's western defenses • Confederates defend capital of Richmond • Union army under McClellan stops Confederate advance into Maryland	• Lincoln issues Emancipation Proclamation, freeing slaves • Confederates defeated at Gettysburg, Pennsylvania; retreat into Virginia • The Union controls Mississippi River • Draft riots in New York and other Northern cities	• Union army under Grant drives Confederate army under Lee deeper into Virginia • Union army under Sherman captures Georgia • Union army under Sheridan captures Shenandoah Valley	• Lee retreats and surrenders at Appomattox • Lincoln assassinated • Andrew Johnson becomes 17th president

MAJOR EVENTS OF THE CIVIL WAR

5. What was the first military action of the Civil War?
(1) the secession of South Carolina from the Union
(2) the Confederate attack on Fort Sumter
(3) the Confederate defense of Richmond
(4) the Confederate advance into Maryland
(5) the Battle of Gettysburg

6. During the Vietnam War, thousands of people participated in public demonstrations to protest the required call-up of young men to serve in the U.S. armed forces. Which event on the timeline was most similar to these demonstrations?
(1) the declaration of war
(2) the secession of most Southern states
(3) the draft riots in Northern cities
(4) the surrender at Appomattox
(5) the assassination of Lincoln

7. How might an official in the Confederate government describe one of the key events of 1861?
(1) South Carolina exercised its sovereign right to ignore national laws.
(2) Six states declared independence from an oppressive government that sought their economic ruin.
(3) Six states withdrew from the United States and sought to destroy the Union.
(4) Union forces valiantly defended Fort Sumter against a brutal Confederate assault.
(5) Union forces invaded Georgia in a destructive march in which they set fire to cities and towns throughout the region.

Questions 8 and 9 refer to the following passage.

During the Middle Ages in Europe, the skilled artisans of each town organized into craft guilds. There were guilds for weavers, cobblers, tanners, and other craftspeople. The craft guilds established monopolies and set wages, standards, prices, and quotas for craft goods. To cut competition, the guilds also put firm limits on the number of craftspeople who could join a guild.

8. The medieval craft guilds are most similar to which modern-day groups?
   (1) consumer protection agencies, which protect consumer interests
   (2) social welfare agencies, which help people with family problems
   (3) tax divisions, which collect income tax, sales tax, and other taxes from citizens
   (4) town councils, which are elected to govern their towns
   (5) professional associations, which set standards and protect members' economic interests

9. What evidence from the paragraph supports the conclusion that a medieval craftsperson might have difficulty getting established in a new town?

   (1) Craft guilds were groups of skilled craftspeople.
   (2) Each craft had its own guild.
   (3) Wages were set by the craft guilds.
   (4) Prices were set by the craft guilds.
   (5) Membership was strictly limited by the guilds.

10. China has the world's oldest continuous civilization. For more than 4,000 years, the Chinese have fought off foreign influences or absorbed them. China's long-running history is due in part to its isolation and distance from other civilizations. The Pacific Ocean to the east, and mountains and deserts to the north, west, and south, protected China for thousands of years.

    What shielded China from outside influences through most of its history?
    (1) geographic barriers and distance from other civilizations
    (2) the ancient roots of its civilization
    (3) its large and powerful army and navy
    (4) the protection of foreign imperialist nations
    (5) a continuous cultural heritage

11. From 1962 to 1992, Algeria was ruled by the army or by one political party—the National Liberation Front (FLN). During this period, foreigners invested in oil and gas, and the economy grew. Slow economic times in the 1980s caused unrest, spurring the government to introduce political reforms. In 1992, it allowed the first multiparty elections. The Islamic Salvation Front won a surprise victory over the FLN. The government declared the election invalid and the army intervened.

    What evidence supports the conclusion that the Algerian government's political reforms were not genuine?
    (1) Foreigners developed Algeria's oil and gas reserves.
    (2) A slow economy led to unrest in Algeria.
    (3) Multiparty elections took place in 1992.
    (4) The Islamic Salvation Front won the elections.
    (5) The government voided the 1992 election results.

Questions 12 and 13 refer to the following map.

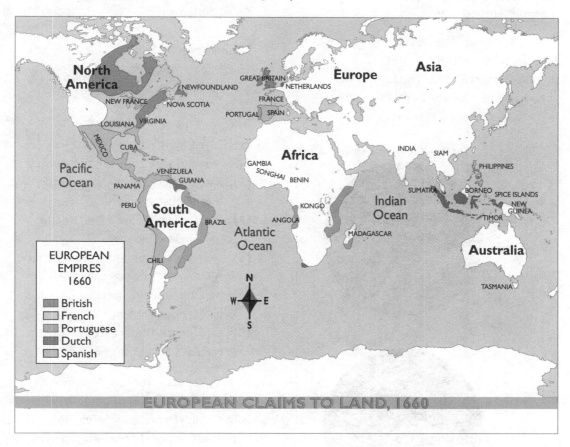

EUROPEAN CLAIMS TO LAND, 1660

12. Which European nation claimed Brazil?
  (1) Great Britain
  (2) France
  (3) Portugal
  (4) The Netherlands
  (5) Spain

13. In 1660, what was the main difference in the locations of Great Britain's and Spain's claims in the Americas?
  (1) Great Britain claimed areas in North America only, and Spain claimed areas on both continents.
  (2) Great Britain claimed areas in South America, and Spain claimed areas in North America.
  (3) Great Britain claimed coastal areas, and Spain claimed inland areas.
  (4) Great Britain claimed inland areas, and Spain claimed coastal areas.
  (5) Great Britain claimed areas on the western coast, and Spain claimed areas on both coasts.

Questions 14 and 15 refer to the following information and graphs.

In 2003, Republican George W. Bush was president. The 108th Congress was divided among Democrats, Republicans, and Independents as shown in these graphs.

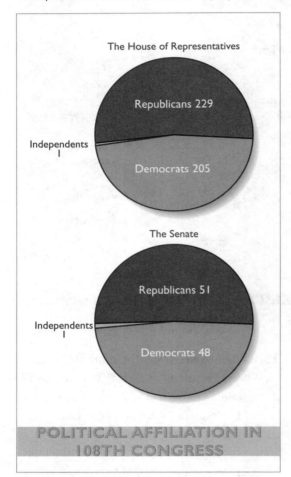

The House of Representatives

Republicans 229

Independents 1

Democrats 205

The Senate

Republicans 51

Independents 1

Democrats 48

POLITICAL AFFILIATION IN 108TH CONGRESS

14. What was the total number of Independents in the 108th Congress?

(1) 1 **(4)** 51

(2) 2 **(5)** 205

(3) 48

15. The vice president gets one vote in case of a tie in the Senate. Why is the vice president's vote unlikely to be needed often in this Congress?

(1) The Republicans have a majority.

(2) The Democrats have a majority.

(3) The Senate has one Independent.

(4) The Senate has 100 members.

(5) The Senate is smaller than the House of Representatives.

16. The First Amendment of the U.S. Constitution says:

"Congress shall make no law respecting an establishment of religion, or prohibiting the free exercise thereof; . . ."

Which of the following actions is prohibited by the clause from the First Amendment that is given above?

(1) meeting in someone's home for a religious ceremony

(2) making one religion the official national religion

(3) giving a sermon in favor of public funding of religious schools

(4) making a public speech against capital punishment

(5) expelling a student from a private religious school for cheating

17. Political socialization is the process by which children learn political values. When children are very young, the most important political figures are police officers and the president. They view both as helpful. By the age of 10 or 11, children in a Democratic household are likely to be critical of a Republican president, and children in a Republican household are likely to be critical of a Democratic president.

Which of the following is evidence for the idea that as children mature, their political beliefs are shaped most strongly by their families?

(1) All children learn political values.

(2) Young children consider police officers important political figures.

(3) Young children look up to a president of any political party.

(4) Children over age 10 whose parents are Democrats are apt to criticize a Republican president.

(5) Both major political parties have organizations for young voters.

Questions 18 and 19 refer to the following cartoon.

Source: Joe Heller/ Greenbay Press-Gazette

18. Who do the people in the cartoon represent?

   (1) Republicans
   (2) Democrats
   (3) politicians
   (4) immigrants
   (5) voters

19. According to the cartoonist, how are negative campaigns effective?

   (1) Voters enjoy negative campaign ads.
   (2) Because of negative campaigning, voters look forward to the end of election season.
   (3) The truth comes out in negative campaign ads.
   (4) Candidates who run negative campaigns win elections.
   (5) Candidates who run negative campaigns are considered mean and nasty.

Questions 20 and 21 refer to the following information and graph.

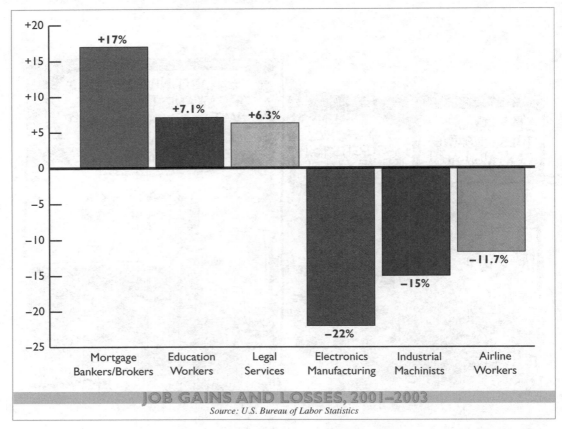

JOB GAINS AND LOSSES, 2001–2003

Source: U.S. Bureau of Labor Statistics

20. Between 2001 and 2003, which job sector lost 11.7 percent of its jobs?

(1) education workers

(2) legal services

(3) electronics manufacturing

(4) industrial machinists

(5) airline workers

21. Which of the following people was most likely to have trouble finding a job during this period?

(1) a loan officer

(2) a teacher

(3) a paralegal

(4) a factory worker

(5) a classroom aide

Question 22 is based on the following chart, which was published in the business section of a Sunday newspaper.

Best National Interest Rates on 5-Year Certificates of Deposit		
Bank	**Minimum Deposit**	**Interest Rate**
Highpoint	$10,000	4.03%
Brandon	$1,000	4.02%
FirstBank	$500	4.00%
CyberBank	$5,000	4.00%

22. Paula wants to invest $750 in a 5-year CD at the best interest rate she can find. Why did Paula select FirstBank?

(1) FirstBank is the only bank to offer 5-year CDs.

(2) FirstBank is the only bank to offer an interest rate of 4.00 percent.

(3) FirstBank is the only bank with a minimum deposit under $1,000.

(4) The other banks have higher interest rates.

(5) The other banks have lower minimum deposits.

Questions 23 and 24 refer to the following map.

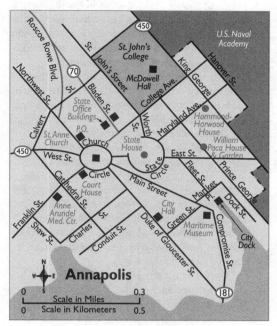

23. Which of the following people would find this map of Annapolis most useful?
    (1) a long-distance trucker
    (2) the city's fire department
    (3) a tourist
    (4) a boater
    (5) a landscape architect

24. Which of the following conclusions is supported by evidence from the map?
    (1) Annapolis is the capital of Maryland.
    (2) Annapolis is Maryland's oldest city.
    (3) Annapolis has Maryland's oldest port.
    (4) Maryland's oldest Catholic church is in Annapolis.
    (5) Annapolis is a relatively small city.

Question 25 refers to the following passage.

The Indus River and its tributaries form the heart of Pakistan, a Muslim nation northwest of India. The Indus flows through the two most populous provinces of Pakistan, the Punjab and Sind.

In the upstream province of Punjab, people speak Punjabi. With irrigation water from the Indus, farmers grow wheat and cotton. People from this region dominate Pakistan's military and government.

Downstream from the Punjab is Sind, a diverse area where many languages are spoken. In recent years, the irrigation canals from the Indus have been low or empty in Sind. A long drought and heavy upstream water use have sharply decreased the water supply. As a result, farmers do not have enough water to raise crops. Much of Sind is turning back into desert.

25. What do the Punjab and Sind have in common?
    (1) Punjabi is the main language.
    (2) Both rely on water from the Indus.
    (3) Both are turning into desert.
    (4) In both, the main crop is wheat.
    (5) Their peoples are leaders in the Pakistani military and government.

Answers and explanations start on page 16.

Social Studies Pretest Answers and Explanations

1. **(4) about 1 in 8** (Comprehension) According to the first paragraph, the typical woman gave birth 5 to 8 times in the colonial period. Over a lifetime, the chance of dying in childbirth was about 1 in 8.

2. **(5) She improved women's chances of surviving childbirth.** (Evaluation) Midwives had knowledge of techniques that aided women in labor. For this reason, the midwife's assistance and availability were highly valued in colonial communities.

3. **(3) the Vietnam War, in which the United States supported South Vietnam against communist North Vietnam** (Application) Although the North Vietnamese eventually won the war, the Vietnam War was fought to contain communism to North Vietnam.

4. **(1) competition** (Evaluation) By restricting trusts, the federal government sought to increase competition.

5. **(2) the Confederate attack on Fort Sumter** (Comprehension) On a timeline, events are arranged in the sequence in which they occurred. Therefore, you need to skim the timeline, starting with 1860, until you find the first <u>military</u> action.

6. **(3) the draft riots in Northern cities** (Application) The informal term referring to the required call-up of people to serve in the armed forces is *the draft.* The timeline indicates that draft riots took place in the North during the Civil War.

7. **(2) Six states declared independence from an oppressive government that sought their economic ruin.** (Analysis) The timeline indicates that in 1861, six Southern states seceded, forming the Confederacy. An official in the Confederate government might describe this event as a declaration of independence similar to the declaration made at the start of the American Revolution.

8. **(5) professional associations, which set standards and protect members' economic interests** (Application) An example of a professional association is the American Medical Association, which certifies and licenses physicians and works in other ways to protect physicians' economic interests.

9. **(5) Membership was strictly limited by the guilds.** (Evaluation) In each town, the craft guilds put a limit on the number of members in order to protect their economic interests and prevent competition.

10. **(1) geographic barriers and distance from other civilizations** (Comprehension) According to the passage, the reason China's civilization has lasted for 4,000 years is because China is far from other centers of civilization and because its geography has helped keep it isolated. The Pacific Ocean, mountains, and deserts provide natural barriers to invasion.

11. **(5) The government voided the 1992 election results.** (Evaluation) If the Algerian government's commitment to political reform had been genuine, it would have allowed the 1992 election results to stand even though the ruling party lost.

12. **(3) Portugal** (Comprehension) First locate Brazil on the map. (It is in South America.) Brazil is green. Look at the key to see which European nation is represented by green.

13. **(1) Great Britain claimed areas in North America only, and Spain claimed areas on both continents.** (Analysis) Locate North and South America. Identify the claims made by Great Britain, which are shown in blue, and Spain, which are shown in pink.

14. **(2) 2** (Comprehension) The first circle graph shows that there was one Independent in the House. The second circle graph shows that there was one Independent in the Senate for a total of two Independents.

15. **(1) The Republicans have a majority.** (Analysis) Votes in both houses of Congress are often along party lines. Since the Republicans have a majority in the Senate, they are likely to win on most issues that come up for a vote. Therefore, the vice president would probably rarely be needed to break a tie vote.

16. **(2) making one religion the official national religion** (Application) The quoted clause states that Congress shall make no laws that would establish an official religion for the country.

17. **(4) Children over age 10 whose parents are Democrats are apt to criticize a Republican president.** (Evaluation) The paragraph indicates that as children mature, they make more judgments about public figures, and these judgments are likely to reflect the political attitudes of their family.

18. **(5) voters** (Comprehension) The people in the cartoon represent ordinary American voters who are watching a campaign ad broadcast on television.

19. **(4) Candidates who run negative campaigns win elections.** (Analysis) The cartoonist indicates that although the voters don't like negative ads, they are still influenced by such ads.

20. **(5) airline workers** (Comprehension) To find the sector that lost 11.7 percent of jobs, look at the three sectors with job losses—the ones with negative percentages, with the bars below zero. Of these, airline workers had a job-loss rate of 11.7 percent.

21. **(4) factory worker** (Application) The graph shows that the two sectors that lost the most jobs were electronics manufacturing and industrial machinists. Both of these are factory-based sectors.

22. **(3) FirstBank is the only bank with a minimum deposit under $1,000.** (Analysis) Paula cannot open a 5-year CD at any of the other banks because these banks require a minimum deposit for 5-year CDs that is higher than the amount of money she wants to invest.

23. **(3) a tourist** (Application) This map is useful for a tourist because it shows museums and historic sites, which would be of interest to a visitor.

24. **(1) Annapolis is the capital of Maryland.** (Evaluation) The map shows that Annapolis is home to Maryland's State House. This is the best evidence that Annapolis serves as Maryland's capital.

25. **(2) Both rely on water from the Indus.** (Analysis) Both provinces need to irrigate the land to grow crops. Irrigation water comes from the Indus River.

Evaluation Charts for Social Studies Pretest

Follow these steps for the most effective use of the Subject Areas and Thinking Skills chart:

- Check your answers against the Answers and Explanations on page 16.
- Use the following charts to circle the questions you answered correctly.
- Total your correct answers in each row (across) for Social Studies subject areas and each column (down) for thinking skills.

You can use the results to determine which subjects you need to focus on.

- The column on the left of the table indicates the KET Pre-GED video program and its corresponding lesson in this workbook.
- The column headings—*Comprehension, Application, Analysis,* and *Evaluation*— refer to the type of thinking skills needed to answer the questions.

SUBJECT AREAS AND THINKING SKILLS

Program	Comprehension (pp. 32–33)	Application (pp. 52–53)	Analysis (pp. 72–73, 92–93)	Evaluation (pp. 112–113)	Total for Subjects
11 U.S. History (pp. 18–37)	1, 5	3, 6	7	2	____/6
12 World History (pp. 38–57)	12	8	13	9, 11	____/5
13 Economics (pp. 58–77)	20	21	22	4	____/4
14 Civics and Government (pp. 78–97)	14, 18	16	15, 19	17	____/6
15 Geography (pp. 58–77)	10	23	25	24	____/4
Total for Skills	____/7	____/6	____/6	____/6	

Many of the questions on the GED Social Studies Test are based on charts, timelines, maps, graphs, and editorial cartoons.

- Use the chart below to circle the graphics-based questions that you answered correctly.
- Identify your strengths and weaknesses in interpreting graphics by counting the number of questions you got correct for each type of graphic.

GRAPHIC SKILLS

Charts and Timelines (p. 34)	Maps (pp. 54, 114)	Graphs (p. 74)	Editorial Cartoons (p. 94)	Total for Graphics
5, 6, 7, 22	12, 13, 23, 24	14, 15, 20, 21	18, 19	____/14

Themes in U.S. History

LESSON GOALS

SOCIAL STUDIES SKILLS

- Understand the birth of the United States and its territorial growth
- Learn how the nation survived a civil war and grew through immigration
- Analyze the effects of wars and social movements on the nation's development

THINKING SKILL

- Comprehend social studies information

GRAPHIC SKILL

- Interpret charts and timelines

GED REVIEW

1. Think About the Topic

The program you are about to watch is about *U.S. History.* Because an understanding of U.S. history is an important part of social studies, U.S. history questions make up about 25 percent of the GED Social Studies Test.

This program is about the history of the United States from the time of the first migrants and settlers up to the present. Learning this history helps you understand how the past affects us today.

To help you see how events are connected in our history, the program will show how the first peoples came to North America and how they, and each group that followed, contributed to the nation we live in.

2. Prepare to Watch the Video

On the program, you will get an overview of U.S. history through interviews with historians. Think about some things you know about the history of the United States.

Name a historical event that happened during your lifetime.

_____

You might have said something like: *I remember the election in the year 2000, when Bush and Gore were the two main presidential candidates.*

3. Preview the Questions

Read the questions under *Think About the Program* on the next page, and keep them in mind as you watch the program. You will review them after you watch.

4. Study the Vocabulary

Review the terms to the right. Understanding the meaning of key social studies vocabulary will help you understand the video and the rest of this lesson.

WATCH THE PROGRAM

As you watch the program, pay special attention to the host who introduces or summarizes major themes in U.S. history that you need to learn about. The host will also give you important information about the GED Social Studies Test.

AFTER YOU WATCH

1. Think About the Program

How did the first Americans reach North America?

What happened when the European explorers arrived?

Why did the English colonists rebel against their king?

How did the nineteenth-century immigrants help shape America?

What major events affected the nation in the twentieth century?

2. Make the Connection

The program talked about the great changes that occurred in the twentieth century. Which change in American life has affected you the most? Explain.

civil rights—the rights and privileges of a citizen

civil war—a war between groups of citizens of the same country

cold war—intense rivalry between nations, stopping short of actual warfare

culture—the way of life of a people, including ideas, religions, customs, and tools

immigrant—a person who moves to another country to start a new life

industrialization— the process of developing factories and other businesses

revolution—the overthrow of an established government by those under its authority

slavery—the practice of owning another human being as a piece of property

technology—the use of scientific knowledge for practical purposes

A New Nation

Native Americans and Settlers

As you learned in the program, America was first settled by people who crossed the Bering Strait from Asia about 30,000 years ago. These migrants spread out across the Americas. They reached every corner of the continent. Adapting themselves to the land, they built shelters from wood, animal hides, adobe, or stone. The rich **cultures** they created reflected the area of the Americas in which each group had settled.

At first, the Native Americans survived by gathering food from the land and hunting wild animals. Then they discovered agriculture. Over time, they developed many varieties of plants for food, including corn.

In 1492, Christopher Columbus sailed across the Atlantic Ocean from Spain, trying to find a new route to India. He stumbled across the islands between North and South America that are now known as the West Indies. Believing he had found India, Columbus called the native people "Indians." Columbus's arrival changed the Americas forever. Over the next centuries, many Europeans came to America, including the Spanish, the French, the English, and the Dutch.

With the meeting of peoples from opposite sides of the Atlantic Ocean came a tremendous exchange of goods and ideas. This exchange came to be called the Columbian Exchange, after Columbus, whose voyage led to the first contact. The chart below gives details of the Columbian Exchange, which had huge effects on all involved. In the Americas, the introduction of the horse allowed Native Americans to travel faster and farther. They began to hunt and conduct wars from horseback. Sadly, the Europeans brought diseases as well. In some areas, measles, typhus, and smallpox killed nearly 90 percent of the Native American population. In Europe, crops from the Americas, including potatoes and corn, soon became staples—basic foods—in people's diets. About 50 percent of the food crops grown in the world today originally came from the Americas.

The Columbian Exchange		
Category	**Americas to Europe, Asia, and Africa**	**Europe, Asia, and Africa to the Americas**
Staples	corn, beans, potato, sweet potato	wheat, oats, barley, rice
Fruits and Vegetables	tomato, pumpkin, squash, peppers, pineapple	bananas, grapes, olives and olive oil, citrus fruit, apples
Livestock	turkeys	horses, sheep, chickens, cows, pigs
Diseases	none known	measles, typhus, smallpox
Miscellaneous	cocoa bean, peanut	sugar, coffee bean

The English Colonies

Colonists from Great Britain first settled along the East Coast of what is now the United States in the 1600s. Some came in search of religious freedom. Others came hoping for wealth. At first, Native Americans and settlers got along well, but soon conflicts began.

The settlers claimed the land they settled as their own. The Native Americans believed the land belonged to everyone. As the settlers pushed west from the coast, fighting between the colonists and the Native Americans became more frequent. The colonists, aided by the British army, drove the Native Americans farther west.

Protecting the colonists forced Great Britain to borrow money. Parliament—the British legislature—increased taxes on the people in Great Britain in order to pay the debt. Then the government decided that the colonists should pay more taxes as well.

The colonists protested that the new taxes were unfair. Tension arose between the colonies and Great Britain and continued to worsen over the years. In 1776, all thirteen colonies signed the **Declaration of Independence.** In this document, they proclaimed their independence from Great Britain. War was declared. In 1781, the American army, under General George Washington, defeated the British at Yorktown, Virginia. The colonies, now the United States of America, had won their independence from Great Britain.

THEMES IN U.S. HISTORY ▪ PRACTICE I

A. Use the chart and information on pages 20 and 21 to complete the sentences.

1. The first settlers in the Americas came from _____.

2. One effect of the Columbian Exchange was the spread of deadly _____ among Native Americans.

3. Because of conflicts with European settlers, Native Americans were forced to move _____.

4. The colonists protested against British _____.

5. The document that proclaimed the colonists' intention to be free was the _____.

B. Use the chart and the information on page 20 to answer the question.

6. Describe two ways in which the Columbian Exchange changed life in the Americas.

_____

_____

Answers and explanations start on page 130.

Creating a Government

As soon as the delegates to the Continental Congress declared their independence in 1776, they created the Articles of Confederation. This first **constitution** of the United States did not provide for a strong central government. Many of America's leaders realized that the Articles had to be fixed—or replaced—if the United States was to succeed as a nation. In 1787, a Constitutional Convention met in Philadelphia.

The delegates to the convention had a difficult task. They had to create a government that was fair to both the small states and the large states. They had to protect the interests of the industrializing North as well as the agricultural South. After much negotiating, the delegates came up with a plan that was acceptable to all parties. The Constitution of the United States of America became the law of the land.

The Nation Grows and Changes

For many years, the United States remained neutral when Europe engaged in wars. In 1803, war broke out between Britain and France. Napoleon Bonaparte, the ruler of France, was in need of money. He offered to sell the Louisiana Territory to the United States for $15 million. President Thomas Jefferson accepted the offer. The **Louisiana Purchase,** as it was called, more than doubled the size of the United States.

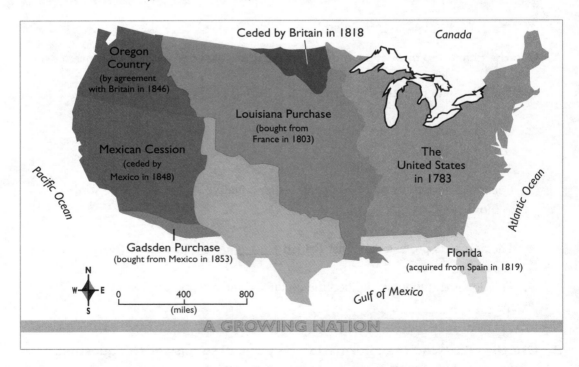

A GROWING NATION

By the beginning of the nineteenth century, the **Industrial Revolution** was changing the United States. Instead of using hand tools to make products at home, workers in factories were operating large machines to manufacture goods. The factory system did not take hold in the agricultural South. Nevertheless, new **technology** had a big impact on that region as well. A machine called the **cotton gin,** invented in the late 1790s, could quickly clean cotton of its sticky seeds. Cotton soon became a very profitable crop on Southern plantations, and its production increased greatly. Consequently, many more workers were needed to pick the cotton. This resulted in an expansion of **slavery.**

In the 1840s, people began to think that the United States had a right to all of the land from the Atlantic coast to the Pacific. This idea became known as **Manifest Destiny,** meaning that occupation of this land by the United States was obviously going to occur.

In 1821, Mexico allowed Americans to settle in Texas. The Americans in Texas fought for and won their independence in 1836. Then, in 1845, Congress allowed Texas into the Union. Mexico was enraged. War between the United States and Mexico began over a border dispute. The United States won an easy victory in the war with Mexico in 1846. Following the war, the United States negotiated to gain all Mexican land north of the Rio Grande, including California. The United States now reached from sea to sea, fulfilling its "manifest destiny."

THEMES IN U.S. HISTORY ▪ PRACTICE 2

A. Use the information on pages 22 and 23 to match each term with its definition.

_____**1.** Articles of Confederation

_____**2.** Louisiana Purchase

_____**3.** Industrial Revolution

_____**4.** Manifest Destiny

a. belief that the United States should reach from the Atlantic coast to the Pacific coast

b. changed the way goods were manufactured

c. first constitution of the United States

d. land sold to the United States by France

B. Answer the questions using the map on page 22 and the information on page 23.

5. After 1803, which three nations were blocking Manifest Destiny? _____

_____

6. Do you think Manifest Destiny was inevitable? Why or why not?

_____

_____

7. How did the growth of technology in the early 1800s affect the North? the South?

_____

_____

Answers and explanations start on page 130.

"Employers are able to expand only insofar as they have enough workers."

A Nation of Immigrants

The Newcomers

As the program mentioned, many people came to America in the nineteenth century. The Industrial Revolution increased the need for workers. When the Irish came to America, they found work in Northern factories. In the West, German and Scandinavian **immigrants** streamed into the newly acquired territories to establish farms.

One group of immigrants was forced to come to America. For several centuries, Africans had been brought here as slaves. Most of them toiled in the cotton fields of the South and were treated as less than human. Their "owners" had absolute power over their lives.

The first half of the nineteenth century saw the rise of **abolitionists.** These reformers worked to end slavery throughout the nation. At the same time, new states were being admitted to the Union. Some were free states, where slavery was not allowed. Others were slave states. Abraham Lincoln was one of a number of people who did not want slavery to spread in the United States. In 1860, after Lincoln was elected president, South Carolina **seceded**, or withdrew, from the Union. The following year, other southern states joined South Carolina to form the Confederate States of America.

Civil War

The Confederacy seized all the U.S. federal buildings, such as post offices, courthouses, and forts, in the South. When Fort Sumter, in South Carolina, refused to surrender to the Confederates, the South fired on it. Thus began the most terrible war in American history, the Civil War.

At first, the war went well for the South. The Confederacy had some of America's finest military officers. The North, on the other hand, had greater resources, as the graphs show. Those resources made the difference; after five long years, the North won the Civil War.

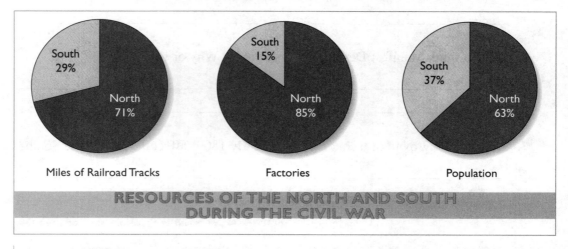

South 29% · North 71% — Miles of Railroad Tracks

South 15% · North 85% — Factories

South 37% · North 63% — Population

RESOURCES OF THE NORTH AND SOUTH DURING THE CIVIL WAR

Reconstruction

During the Civil War, Lincoln issued the **Emancipation Proclamation,** which freed all slaves in the Confederate states. The proclamation had little effect, because the Confederate states were not under Union control. But when the North won the war, nearly four million slaves in the South gained their freedom. The era of **Reconstruction**—rebuilding—began.

On April 14, 1865, Lincoln was assassinated. Andrew Johnson, the vice-president, became president. One of Johnson's first acts was to call for the states to accept the **Thirteenth Amendment,** which outlawed slavery in the United States. However, Johnson was a Southerner, and he did not want to further punish the defeated South.

A group in Congress, known as the **Radical Republicans**, disagreed about further punishment for the South. They proposed the **Fourteenth Amendment,** which made citizens of all persons born in the United States. This included most former slaves. In 1869, the **Fifteenth Amendment** gave all African-American men over the age of 21 the right to vote in federal elections.

These new laws angered many white Southerners. To regain political control, some whites terrorized former slaves and would not allow them to exercise their right to vote. These and other racial problems continued well into the twentieth century.

THEMES IN U.S. HISTORY ▪ PRACTICE 3

A. Study pages 24 and 25. Then put a check mark next to each <u>true</u> statement.

_____ **1.** Supporters of the expansion of slavery into new states were called abolitionists.

_____ **2.** The Southern states joined together to form the Confederate States of America.

_____ **3.** The North had an advantage in the Civil War because it had greater resources than the South.

_____ **4.** The rebuilding of the Union after the Civil War was known as secession.

B. Answer the following questions using the information on pages 24 and 25.

5. List two ways the North's superior resources probably helped it win the Civil War.

_____

_____

6. What were some problems faced by newly freed African Americans in the South?

_____

_____

Answers and explanations start on page 130.

Creating a World Power

After the Civil War, immigrants fleeing poverty and persecution began to arrive from eastern and southern Europe. Large numbers of Asians began arriving on the West Coast. These new immigrants were not as readily accepted as those who had come earlier in the century. Many spoke little or no English. Their customs were different from those of average Americans. They were often the victims of prejudice.

America needed workers, however, and the immigrants were vital to the growing strength of the nation. Great industries like steel, oil, and the railroads were created by the labor of immigrants. The **transcontinental railroad,** which linked the East and West coasts, was an example of the work of these new Americans. Irish and other laborers started in the east; Asian and other laborers started in the west. The two groups laid the tracks that met in Utah in 1869. The railroad was a major factor in America becoming a world economic power. It allowed Americans to move resources and products easily all across the country and subsequently to foreign markets.

The second half of the nineteenth century was a time of great scientific creativity. New inventions, including those listed on the timeline, changed life in the United States.

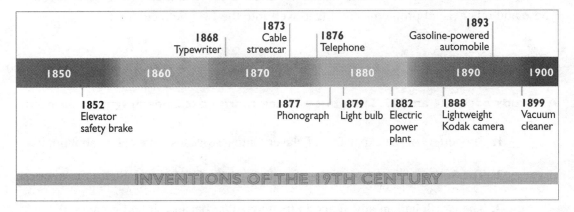

1868 Typewriter
1873 Cable streetcar
1876 Telephone
1893 Gasoline-powered automobile

1850 1860 1870 1880 1890 1900

1852 Elevator safety brake
1877 Phonograph
1879 Light bulb
1882 Electric power plant
1888 Lightweight Kodak camera
1899 Vacuum cleaner

INVENTIONS OF THE 19TH CENTURY

The nation's growth brought many changes. In 1860, only 20 percent of the population lived in cities. By 1900, 40 percent of the population was urban. Much of the increase was due to immigration. The poorer sections of many cities became slums, where families lived in buildings called **tenements.** Conditions in housing and industry drew the attention of journalists called **muckrakers.** Writers like Jacob Riis, Ida Tarbell, and Upton Sinclair exposed social injustices and the greed of industry's "robber barons." Reformers called **Progressives** demanded changes in the way America did business and treated its poor.

As the United States became an economic power, it began to compete with Europe in the race for colonies. Many Americans felt that the nation needed colonies as markets for its products. This desire to control weaker countries is called **imperialism.** The first Pacific territory the United States acquired was Alaska, in 1867. Although at the time considered a bad bargain, it proved a rich source of natural resources. Then, in 1893, Queen Liliuokalani of Hawaii tried to reduce the power and influence of the American planters on the islands. The planters persuaded the U.S. government that they were in danger. A U.S. warship stood by as the planters overthrew the queen. Hawaii was annexed by Congress in 1898.

In 1898, a **revolution** in Cuba sparked the Spanish-American War. After the war, which lasted a mere four months, the United States acquired the Philippines, Puerto Rico, and Cuba.

When Theodore Roosevelt became president, he wanted to build a canal to connect the Atlantic Ocean and Pacific Ocean. He acquired the rights to build this canal across the isthmus of Panama, a narrow strip of land in Central America. The Panama Canal took nearly ten years to build. It was completed in 1914 and became a major factor in international trade.

THEMES IN U.S. HISTORY ▪ PRACTICE 4

A. Study pages 26 and 27. Then complete each sentence by circling the letter of the correct answer.

1. A major factor in America becoming an economic power was the building of the
   a. tenements   **b.** transcontinental railroad   **c.** cable streetcars   **d.** Alaska pipeline

2. New immigrants from eastern and southern Europe were often victims of
   a. prejudice   **b.** muckrakers   **c.** imperialists   **d.** international trade

3. All of the following inventions changed life in the nineteenth century except the
   a. typewriter   **b.** phonograph   **c.** personal computer   **d.** light bulb

4. Social injustice and the greed of robber barons were exposed by writers called
   a. muckrakers   **b.** imperialists   **c.** immigrants   **d.** Progressives

5. The desire of a powerful country to control weaker countries is called
   a. Progressivism   **b.** abolition   **c.** secession   **d.** imperialism

6. The overthrow of Queen Liliuokalani eventually resulted in the annexation of
   a. Cuba   **b.** Hawaii   **c.** the Philippines   **d.** Alaska

7. A narrow strip of land that separates two bodies of water is called a(n)
   a. continent   **b.** island   **c.** peninsula   **d.** isthmus

B. Use the timeline on page 26 to answer the questions.

8. Which invention of the nineteenth century made it practical to build skyscrapers?

   _____

9. Which invention of the nineteenth century do you think affected the most people? Explain.

   _____

   _____

Answers and explanations start on page 130.

"[The twentieth century] was a century of incredible changes and events."

A Nation of Change

World War I

In 1914, a world war broke out in Europe between the **Central Powers** (Germany, Austria-Hungary, and Italy) and the **Allied Powers** (France, Great Britain, and Russia). At first, the United States was neutral. However, the loss of American lives in German attacks on Allied passenger ships led to strong anti-German feelings in America. The United States declared war on Germany in 1917. About two million American soldiers went to fight in Europe. Together with British and French troops, they forced the Germans to retreat. On November 11, 1918, World War I ended.

President Wilson did not want the Allies to punish Germany too harshly. However, the Treaty of Versailles, of 1919, was designed to weaken Germany. It required Germany to pay billions of dollars in reparations and strictly limited the size of Germany's military.

Wilson did succeed in establishing the **League of Nations**, which was similar to today's United Nations. The Allies joined the League, but Wilson could not persuade the United States to join. As a result, the League was doomed to eventual failure.

In the 1920s, the American economy boomed. Factories nearly doubled their prewar production. As automobiles became popular and affordable, other industries grew. The increase in automobile production created a need for more steel, rubber, and paved roads.

The early 1900s was also a time of great social change. In 1920, the **Nineteenth Amendment** gave women the right to vote. Radio and the movies contributed to the development of mass culture, and African-American musicians created a new kind of music called jazz.

In 1929, the stock market crashed, and the nation plunged into the Great Depression. Unemployment soared, and a drought in the West brought ruin to many farmers.

U.S. Unemployment (1929–1944)		
Year	Estimated Number of People Unemployed	Percentage of Labor Force
1929	1,555,000	3.2
1931	8,020,000	15.9
1933	12,830,000	24.9
1935	10,610,000	20.1
1937	7,700,000	14.3
1938	10,390,000	19.0
1940	8,120,000	14.6
1942	2,260,000	4.7
1944	670,000	1.2

Source: U.S. Bureau of the Census

Another World War

In 1932, Franklin D. Roosevelt was elected president, promising a "new deal" for the American people. Roosevelt began pushing his programs through Congress. Millions of dollars in government funds were spent on relief and on efforts to end the depression.

In Germany, Adolf Hitler rose to power by exploiting Germans' resentment of the Treaty of Versailles. In 1938, Germany began taking over neighboring countries. The **Axis** powers—Germany, Italy, and Japan—threatened the world. The **Allied** powers—Britain and France—declared war on Germany in 1939. France fell to the Germans the following year. In 1942, Japan attacked the U.S. fleet at Pearl Harbor, Hawaii, which drew America into the war. Britain, the United States, and the Soviet Union led the war against the Axis.

War production restored the U.S. economy as planes, tanks, and ships rolled off assembly lines. World War II was fought throughout the world. At first the war went badly for the Allies. Then the Allies defeated German forces in North Africa and Italy. British and American forces next recaptured France. By May 1945, the Allies had won the war in Europe.

In the Pacific, the war was fought island by island. By 1945, the Allies were preparing to invade Japan. Unknown to the rest of the world, the United States had developed an **atomic bomb.** President Harry Truman ordered the bomb to be dropped on two Japanese cities, Hiroshima and Nagasaki. The bomb's power stunned the Japanese. They quickly surrendered, ending World War II.

THEMES IN U.S. HISTORY ▪ PRACTICE 5

A. Use the information on pages 28 and 29 to complete each sentence.

1. The _____ punished Germany for its role in World War I.

2. The _____ guaranteed women the right to vote.

3. The first organization to attempt forming an international government was the _____.

4. World War II ended when the United States dropped _____ on Hiroshima and Nagasaki.

B. Choose the best answer based on the chart and information on pages 28 and 29.

5. What was the trend in the unemployment rate during the Great Depression?
   a. It rose steadily.   **b.** It dropped steadily.   **c.** It rose and fell and rose and fell.

6. How would the unemployment rate have affected consumer spending during the Great Depression?   **a.** increased it   **b.** decreased it   **c.** had no effect

Answers and explanations start on page 131.

The Cold War

The Soviet Union was a **communist** nation; this meant that the government owned all of the land and industries, and the Communist Party controlled the government. When World War II ended, Soviet soldiers occupied most of Eastern Europe. By seizing control of the governments of Eastern European nations, the Soviet Union created **satellite nations** that it could dominate. So Europe quickly became divided between democracies in the west and communist nations in the east. The dividing line was called the **iron curtain.**

Tensions developed between the communist and democratic nations, especially between the United States and the Soviet Union. This tension led to the **Cold War**—an intense rivalry stopping short of military conflict. In the second half of the twentieth century, the cold war dominated international relations. An arms race developed between the two **superpowers,** as each nation tried to outdo the other in producing weapons. Wars related to cold war tensions broke out in several places, including Korea and Vietnam. The timeline below chronicles some of the many confrontations that occurred during the Cold War, as well as some of the attempts to achieve peace.

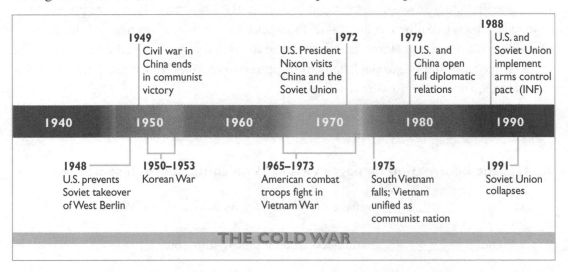

Meanwhile, social changes were taking place in America. African Americans, women, Native Americans, and Latinos began to demand their **civil rights**. Asian Americans and other ethnic groups fought against discrimination.

In 1957, the Soviets launched *Sputnik*, a small space satellite, into orbit around Earth. Americans felt embarrassed that the Soviets had beaten them into space. In 1960, under President John F. Kennedy, America began a space program that landed an astronaut on the moon in 1969.

President Ronald Reagan, elected in 1980, intensified the cold war arms race. Increased spending on arms by the United States forced the Soviet Union to increase its military budget as well. This contributed to its already disastrous economic problems, and the Soviet Union collapsed in 1991. This ended the Cold War, which had spanned 46 years of the twentieth century.

A New Era

The 1990s ushered in a period of economic growth. The boom was fueled by consumer spending, much of it on technology products. The personal computer, which had become a common household item by 1990, contributed to a widespread technological revolution.

The Internet began in 1969 as a U.S. Department of Defense project that linked the computers of four universities. Civilian use of the Internet began to grow in 1991. By the beginning of 2002, there were over 38 million Web sites worldwide. One result of this technology has been the rapid spread of information all over the world.

The world was shocked on September 11, 2001, when terrorists made simultaneous attacks on the World Trade Center in New York and the Pentagon in Washington, D.C. As a result of these attacks, the United States launched a "war on terror." The September 11th attacks caused Americans to ask difficult questions: How can we balance our freedom and our safety? How can we work with other nations to promote and protect democracy? How can we help bring an end to the hunger, poverty, and despair that inspire people to take up ideologies of desperation and hate? How can we resolve our differences peacefully and with justice for all? Our answers to these questions will shape the future of our nation and our world.

THEMES IN U.S. HISTORY ▪ PRACTICE 6

A. Using the timeline and the information on pages 30 and 31, put the events in chronological order from earliest to latest.

_____ **1.** The Soviet Union collapsed.

_____ **2.** The United States and Communist China began full diplomatic relations.

_____ **3.** The World Trade Center and the Pentagon were attacked by terrorists.

_____ **4.** The Soviet Union took over the governments of Eastern European nations.

_____ **5.** The United States sent its first combat troops to Vietnam.

_____ **6.** The Korean War ended.

_____ **7.** Vietnam became a communist nation.

_____ **8.** The United States stopped the Soviets from taking control of West Berlin.

_____ **9.** A U.S. astronaut landed on the moon.

B. Use the information on pages 30 and 31 to answer the following questions.

10. How did the arms race ultimately affect the Soviet Union?

_____

_____

Answers and explanations start on page 131.

Comprehend Social Studies Materials

When you **comprehend** what you read, you understand its meaning. You understand the main point and any supporting facts or details.

On the GED Social Studies Test, some questions will test whether you understand social studies concepts. You may be asked to find specific information or to summarize or restate facts. You may also have to figure out some information that is only suggested in a passage.

When you **comprehend** something, you understand what is stated in the text or shown in a picture. You may need to restate a fact using other words or summarize a passage or a graphic. You may also need to **infer**—figure out something that is suggested but not directly stated.

EXAMPLE

Construction of the Erie Canal, which connected the Hudson River and Lake Erie, began in 1817. It was a difficult project. Upper New York State has many landforms that challenged the canal's engineers. The Montezuma Swamp, a marsh near Syracuse, was one problem. Building the canal over the powerful Genesee River at Rochester was another. At the Niagara Escarpment, a high cliff, the engineers designed locks to move boats up or down the 70 feet from the top to the bottom. When the canal was completed, shipping goods from the Midwest became faster and cheaper. A ton of grain could travel from the Midwest to New York City in 6 days instead of 20.

1. List three landforms that challenged the Erie Canal's engineers.

_____

Did you say *the Montezuma Swamp, the Genesee River,* and *the Niagara Escarpment?* If so, you are correct.

THINKING STRATEGY: When a GED question asks you about a specific fact in a passage, quickly skim the passage to find the word or phrase. Then reread the entire sentence or sentences with the word or phrase to figure out the answer.

2. What effect did the Erie Canal have on the economy of New York City?

_____

If you said something like *New York City became an important trade center for Midwestern farmers*, you are right. You made an inference based on the passage. The Erie Canal allowed Midwestern farmers to ship their crops easily to New York City.

Now let's look at some comprehension questions similar to those on the GED Test.

Sample GED Question

Today's political campaigns have their roots in the "Log Cabin" campaign of 1840. Whig presidential candidate William Henry Harrison had no outstanding qualifications, so the Whigs provided him with an image: they claimed Harrison had been born in a log cabin and had made his way up in the world. In fact, he had been born into a wealthy family. His opponent, Martin Van Buren, was pictured as an aristocrat, although he had not grown up in wealth. The image making was successful, and Harrison won the election.

Which statement summarizes this information?
(1) William Henry Harrison was a great politician.
(2) Whig Party members believed in their candidate's qualifications.
(3) Modern political image making began in 1840.
(4) Political parties always lie about their candidates.
(5) Martin Van Buren was defeated in spite of being the better candidate.

THINKING STRATEGY: A **summary** is a brief statement of a passage's main point. It is often found in the topic sentence. Look for the topic sentence in the paragraph above.

The correct answer is **(3) Modern political image making began in 1840.**
The answer is correct because it sums up the paragraph, restating the first sentence—the topic sentence.

GED THINKING SKILL PRACTICE • COMPREHENSION

Questions 1 and 2 are based on the passage below.

Abigail Adams was a strong-minded woman. She had little formal education, but she was well-read. John Adams, her husband, was a leader of the move for independence and was rarely home. Abigail ran the farm and raised the children. However, her thoughts often focused on issues under discussion at the Continental Congress. In 1776, she wrote to John, who was a delegate to the Continental Congress: "Remember the Ladies, and be more generous . . . to them. . . . Do not put unlimited power into the hands of the Husbands."

1. Based on the passage, you can infer that Abigail Adams wanted
(1) her husband to write back
(2) more rights for women
(3) a generous present from her husband
(4) unlimited power
(5) to attend the Congress

2. Which statement best summarizes the information about Abigail Adams?
(1) She was a good farmer.
(2) She was well educated.
(3) She was a smart and capable woman.
(4) She disliked the British.
(5) She resented John's political success.

Answers and explanations start on page 131.

Understand Charts and Timelines

On the GED Social Studies Test, you will have to interpret charts and timelines. Charts organize information of different types. Timelines show the order in which events occurred.

EXAMPLE

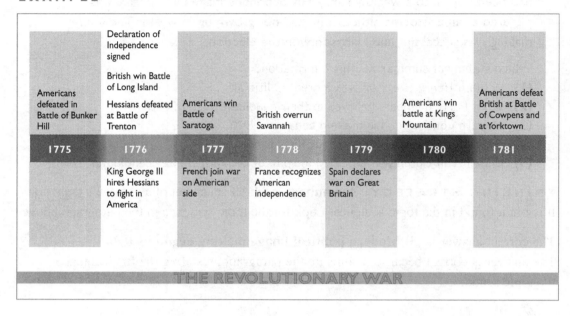

Americans defeated in Battle of Bunker Hill

Declaration of Independence signed

British win Battle of Long Island

Hessians defeated at Battle of Trenton

Americans win Battle of Saratoga

British overrun Savannah

Americans win battle at Kings Mountain

Americans defeat British at Battle of Cowpens and at Yorktown

1775 · 1776 · 1777 · 1778 · 1779 · 1780 · 1781

King George III hires Hessians to fight in America

French join war on American side

France recognizes American independence

Spain declares war on Great Britain

THE REVOLUTIONARY WAR

1. In what year did the Revolutionary War begin? _____

Did you say *1775?* If so, you are right. The title of the timeline is "The Revolutionary War." The first entry on the timeline is the first major battle of the war, the Battle of Bunker Hill. This timeline covers the entire period of the war. Notice that the timeline has intervals of one year.

THINKING STRATEGY: Look at the entries above and below the line. The events above the line occurred in the American colonies. The events below the line occurred in Europe. To fully understand this timeline, look for relationships between the events above and below the timeline.

2. What events in Europe helped the colonists win the Revolutionary War, and when did they occur?

_____

_____

Your answer should be: *The French joined the colonists' side of the war in 1777, and the Spanish joined the war against the British in 1779.* Based on the timeline, you can infer that these decisions by European powers affected what happened later in America.

Now let's look at some more questions similar to those you will see on the GED Test.

GED Chart Practice

America's First National Parks			
Name	**Year Established**	**State**	**Main Attractions**
Yellowstone	1872	WY, ID, MT	World's most abundant geysers
Yosemite	1890	CA	Mountains, gorges, and waterfalls
Sequoia	1890	CA	Giant sequoia trees and mountains
Mt. Rainier	1899	WA	Stunning mountain peak and forests
Crater Lake	1902	OR	Deep blue lake in volcanic crater
Wind Cave	1903	SD	Limestone caves; buffalo herd
Mesa Verde	1906	CO	Prehistoric cliff dwellings

Which two National Parks were established in 1890?

(1) Yellowstone and Yosemite

(2) Yellowstone and Sequoia

(3) Yosemite and Sequoia

(4) Sequoia and Mt. Rainier

(5) Mt. Rainier and Wind Cave

THINKING STRATEGY: First locate the column in the chart that gives the year in which each park was established. Then read down that column to find the year 1890. Read across to the left to see which two parks were established in that year.

The correct answer is **(3) Yosemite and Sequoia.** The chart indicates that these parks were established in 1890. They were America's second and third National Parks. Yellowstone, established in 1872, was the first National Park.

GED GRAPHIC SKILL PRACTICE

USING CHARTS

Questions 1 and 2 are based on the information and the chart below.

The death toll in World War II reflected not only the loss of military personnel, but also the death of civilians. The war was fought in Europe, Africa, and in Asia. Except for the Japanese attack on Pearl Harbor in Hawaii, however, no enemy military action took place on U.S. soil. The chart shows the death toll for the main countries involved in the war.

Deaths During World War II	
Country	**Military and Civilian Deaths**
France	592,000
Germany	5,600,000
Great Britain	366,400
Italy	286,900
Japan	2,133,400
Soviet Union	17,700,000
United States	405,400

Source: World War II: A Statistical Survey, *by John Ellis*

1. An alternative title for this chart is
   (1) Military Action in World War II
   (2) Japanese Losses in the World Wars
   (3) Allied Losses in World War II
   (4) European Losses in World War II
   (5) The Human Cost of World War II
   the Nile River

2. Which country suffered the most losses?
   (1) Germany
   (2) Japan
   (3) Great Britain
   (4) the Soviet Union
   (5) the United States

Answers and explanations start on page 131.

GED Review: U.S. History

Choose the <u>one best answer</u> to the questions below.

<u>Questions 1 and 2</u> refer to the following paragraph and chart.

In the election of 1824, there was only one political party, the Jeffersonian Republicans. The party nominated four candidates: Andrew Jackson, John Quincy Adams, William Crawford, and Henry Clay. Jackson won more votes than any one of the other candidates. However, he did not have the majority of the Electoral College votes. Under these circumstances, the president is chosen by the House of Representatives. Each state had one vote. Only the top three candidates were eligible, so Clay was eliminated. Crawford became very ill and dropped out. As Speaker of the House, Clay had influence. He urged the members of the House who had supported him to vote for Adams.

Candidate	Electoral Vote	Popular Vote	House Vote
Jackson	99	153,544	7
Adams	84	108,740	13
Crawford	41	46,618	4
Clay	37	47,136	–

1. The presidential election of 1824 was more complicated than many other elections. What can you infer caused the complications with this election?
   (1) There were no voting machines at the time.
   (2) Four candidates competed in the election.
   (3) None of the candidates was popular.
   (4) Henry Clay was eliminated.
   (5) The candidates campaigned badly.

2. Based on the paragraph and the chart, what can you infer was the outcome of the 1824 presidential election?
   (1) Clay won the popular vote.
   (2) Crawford won enough electoral votes to become president.
   (3) Adams won because he was Speaker of the House.
   (4) Adams won because Clay got many House members to vote for Adams.
   (5) Jackson lost the popular vote and so did not win the presidency.

<u>Question 3</u> refers to the paragraph below.

The Africans who came to the American colonies as slaves in 1619 often were granted rights or some freedoms. Sometimes they could choose the type of work they did. In Virginia, they could work in a city and send their wages to the owners on the plantations. Then, in the eighteenth century, slaves became vital to running the Southern plantations. In colonies like South Carolina, slaves were 75 percent of the population. As the number of slaves increased, slave codes were written. These laws deprived people who were enslaved of their most basic rights.

3. Which of the following statements is a summary of the passage?
   (1) As the number of slaves increased, their lives became easier.
   (2) Slaves often bought their freedom.
   (3) Slaves always demanded their rights.
   (4) Slaves lost what rights they had as their numbers increased.
   (5) Slaves were well paid in the eighteenth century.

Questions 4 and 5 refer to the following paragraph and timeline.

Although African Americans had been granted citizenship and the right to vote in the nineteenth century, they did not enjoy equal rights with whites. In many places, laws kept the races separate. By the 1960s, the civil rights movement had gained many victories, and discriminatory laws were overturned. However, even then, few could imagine that one day an African American would be honored by a national holiday.

1954—	Supreme Court bans segregation in public schools in *Brown* v. *Board of Education*
1964—	Congress passes Civil Rights Act to outlaw segregation in public places and job discrimination
1965—	Civil rights demonstrators beaten in march in Selma, Alabama
1967—	Thurgood Marshall named first African American Supreme Court Justice
1986—	Birthday of Dr. Martin Luther King, Jr. becomes national holiday

4. A good title for the timeline would be
   (1) Civil Rights in the Nineteenth Century
   (2) Historical Events of the 1960s
   (3) The Struggle for Civil Rights
   (4) The Career of Thurgood Marshall
   (5) The Life of Martin Luther King, Jr.

5. Which two methods directly struck down discriminatory laws?
   (1) public demonstrations and marches
   (2) Supreme Court decisions and public demonstrations
   (3) public demonstrations and acts of Congress
   (4) Supreme Court decisions and acts of Congress
   (5) marches and national holidays

Question 6 refers to the paragraph below.

During World War II, over 150,000 women served in the armed forces, for example, as pilots in the Women's Air Force Service Pilots (WASP) division. WASP fliers received the same training as men. However, they were not trained for combat. Their job was to fly transports, fighter planes, and bombers in noncombat situations. Many women were decorated for their service in the war.

6. Which of the following statements is a summary of the passage?
   (1) Women are better workers than men.
   (2) Women pilots took on noncombat duties during World War II.
   (3) Women should not do men's jobs.
   (4) Everyone worked for the armed forces during World War II.
   (5) WASP fliers could not have learned how to shoot guns.

Question 7 refers to the following graph.

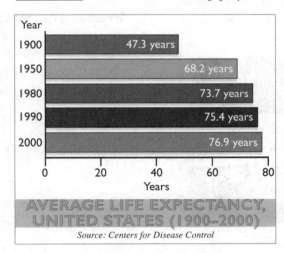

AVERAGE LIFE EXPECTANCY, UNITED STATES (1900–2000)
Source: Centers for Disease Control

7. Based on the graph, when were the greatest gains in life expectancy made?
   (1) before 1900
   (2) between 1900 and 1950
   (3) between 1950 and 1980
   (4) between 1980 and 1990
   (5) between 1990 and 2000

Answers and explanations start on page 131.

Themes in World History

LESSON GOALS

SOCIAL STUDIES SKILLS

- Understand how civilizations and empires developed
- Trace events that helped lead to the rise of nations
- Analyze how developments in industry, transportation, and communication have changed and continue to change the world

THINKING SKILL

- Apply social studies information

GRAPHIC SKILL

- Interpret maps

GED REVIEW

1. Think About the Topic

The program you are about to watch is about *World History*. Americans share Earth with the people of the rest of the world. If you are to understand the world, you must know its history. For that reason, world history is part of the GED Social Studies Test.

This program is about the history of the world, from the time of the first civilizations to the present. Learning this history helps you recognize connections, changes, and patterns of events that make both the past and the present more understandable.

The program will show how people first came to live in groups, how early civilizations spread, and how ideas and inventions changed the world.

2. Prepare to Watch the Video

The program will give you an overview of world history. Think about some things you know about a country that one or more of your ancestors came from.

What is the name of that country? _____

Write something you know about the country. _____

_____

You might have said something like: *My ancestors came from India. It is the largest country in South Asia.*

3. Preview the Questions

Read the questions under *Think About the Program* on the next page, and keep them in mind as you watch the program. You will review them after you watch.

4. Study the Vocabulary

Review the terms to the right. Understanding the meaning of key social studies vocabulary will help you understand the video and the rest of this lesson.

WATCH THE PROGRAM

As you watch the program, listen for the major themes in world history. Also look for helpful information you can use when you take the GED Social Studies Test.

AFTER YOU WATCH

1. Think About the Program

Where did civilizations first arise? Why did they arise there?

List some accomplishments of the Chinese, the Greeks, and the Romans during the period known as the Classical Era.

When was the Renaissance, and what were some great Renaissance achievements in the arts?

Why was the printing press very important in world history?

What social changes occurred because of the Industrial Revolution?

How did electricity affect life in the twentieth century?

2. Make the Connection

The twentieth century has been a time of rapid scientific and technological change. What do you think has been the most important change during your lifetime? Explain.

TERMS

civilization—a form of culture characterized by cities, complex political and social institutions, advanced technologies, and a system of record keeping

dynasty—a series of rulers from a single family

empire—a political unit having a large territory or comprising a number of territories and which is ruled by a single ruler

feudalism—a system in which people are given land in return for service to a king, queen, or person of noble status

globalization—the process of making something global in scope, so that it applies or relates to the entire Earth

imperialism—the policy by which a nation dominates other nations or regions politically, economically, and/ or militarily

Industrial Revolution—the shift that began in Great Britain in the 1700s from home-based hand manufacturing to large-scale factory production

nationalism—the belief that people should focus their loyalty on their nation

renaissance—rebirth of learning

surplus—being in excess of what is needed or required

"Many ideas that are still important to us today date to some of the world's earliest civilizations."

Civilizations to Empires

As you learned in the program, the earliest **civilizations** grew up around rivers, where rich soil along the riverbanks made farming possible. Farmers could live close to one another. They no longer had to spread out to hunt or to gather food. These early civilizations shared several common features:

- Advanced cities, each serving as a center for regional trade
- Specialized workers, such as farmers, craftspeople, traders, scribes, and priests
- Complex institutions, including government and organized religion
- Record keeping, such as a system of writing or a calendar to keep track of time
- Advanced technology, such as plows, irrigation systems, metalworking, or sails

The first known civilization was Sumer, which arose around 3500 B.C. It developed in Mesopotamia, in the region that today is called the Middle East. Two rivers flow through this area, the Tigris and the Euphrates. Every year, these rivers flooded. When the floodwaters receded, a rich layer of mud was left behind. Crops grew well in this soil. However, as you learned in the video, the rivers were unpredictable. Because of this, the Sumerians worked together to build flood-control and irrigation systems. With these systems in place, the Sumerians grew **surplus** crops. They could trade their extra food for wood, stone, and other building materials they needed. Soon cities arose in Mesopotamia, each controlled by a local leader, who was usually a priest. Each city had a stepped pyramid, called a ziggurat, at its center. Here, the priest conducted rituals, planned building projects, and stored harvested crops. Detailed descriptions of Sumerian cities survive and have been translated from the ancient **cuneiform** writing.

Another ancient civilization began in Egypt, along the banks of the Nile River around 3100 B.C. Unlike the Tigris and Euphrates in Mesopotamia, the Nile's yearly floods were predictable. Farmers along its banks produced surplus crops, which led to the rise of trade and the growth of cities. Over time a line of powerful kings, called **pharaohs**, took control of the Nile River valley. The pharaohs used slave labor to build huge tombs called pyramids. These have survived to this day, along with many examples of ancient Egyptian writing, called **hieroglyphics**. We've learned about Egypt's rich history by studying the pyramids and other artifacts and by translating hieroglyphics.

In the Indus River valley in what is today Pakistan, an ancient civilization emerged around 2500 B.C. As with Mesopotamia and Egypt, cities developed along the riverbanks. However, the Indus Valley cities were different from those in the civilizations to the west. They were not haphazard but laid out on a precise grid. Buildings were made of standard-sized bricks. Each neighborhood had a well, and individual houses had their own plumbing. (Such luxuries were not common again until the late 1800s.) Examples of writing have been found but have not yet been deciphered.

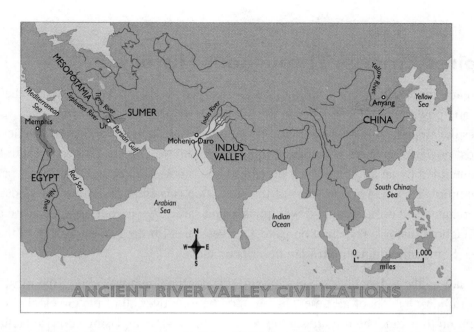

ANCIENT RIVER VALLEY CIVILIZATIONS

China's ancient civilization emerged along the Yellow River and in other river valley sites around 2000 B.C. These rivers deposited rich soil along their banks, making agriculture possible. In time, surplus crops led to the growth of cities. Some cities were surrounded by huge earthen walls that could have only been built by a labor force of thousands. No written records have survived from China's earliest years. But there are numerous written records from around 1700 B.C. Chinese writing helped bring together many ethnic groups because it was a system of **pictographs,** or pictures representing objects or ideas. Although the ethnic groups spoke different languages, the written language was the same throughout China. The pictographic writing helped unify Chinese civilization.

THEMES IN WORLD HISTORY ▪ PRACTICE I

A. Use the map above to match each civilization with the river(s) it was centered on. You will need to use one civilization from the list more than once.

_____ **1.** Euphrates River   **a.** China

_____ **2.** Indus River   **b.** Egypt

_____ **3.** Nile River   **c.** Indus Valley

_____ **4.** Tigris River   **d.** Sumer

_____ **5.** Yellow River

B. Use the information on pages 40 and 41 to answer the following question.

6. Why did early civilizations grow up around large rivers?

_____

_____

Answers and explanations start on page 132.

Empires Emerge Throughout History

As the early civilizations grew, strong leaders emerged. In their desire to expand their wealth and power, these leaders began to conquer other peoples. In this way, vast **empires** developed, spreading their culture, language, and religion to distant peoples. The most powerful empires had several things in common. They had a strong central government led by an emperor. They organized communication between different parts of the empire. They had good means of transportation (via ships and often via roads) so that merchants and armies could travel quickly and safely. Numerous empires arose and fell throughout history. The chart on page 43 gives dates for the longest lasting of these empires. Some important empires are described below.

As you saw in the video, Greek conqueror Alexander the Great was one of the most famous military leaders of all times. In 336 B.C., he took over all of the Greek city-states and went on to invade the mightiest empire of the time—Persia. Using surprise tactics, Alexander quickly routed the huge Persian army. He also conquered Egypt and the Indus Valley. Although Alexander died young and his empire was split among his three most powerful generals, the Greeks had a huge influence over the vast lands Alexander had conquered. A blend of Greek, Egyptian, Persian, and Indian cultures, the **Hellenistic** culture advanced science, philosophy, and art. Huge cities, where people of many different cultures mixed, were centers of international trade. A dialect of Greek called koine allowed diverse peoples to communicate and ideas to flow throughout the empire.

Another Mediterranean civilization started to expand as Hellenistic culture went into decline. This civilization centered on the city of Rome. By around 150 B.C., the Romans had gained control of the land circling the Mediterranean Sea. They went on to take control of much of Europe. At the height of the Roman Empire, from 27 B.C. to A.D. 180, 80 million people lived peacefully together under Roman rule. A huge system of roads and vast trading networks connected the empire. Trade routes, including the Silk Road, linked Rome even to far-off India and China. Rome was the site of great architecture and accomplished engineering feats that people still admire today.

Religion was the force uniting the Islamic Empire (750 to 1258), which stretched from the Indus Valley, through today's Middle East, across northern Africa, to Spain. Arabic was the common language, and the dinar was the common coin. Banks issued notes of credit (the origin of our bank checks) that were honored throughout the large empire. Therefore, trade flourished along both land and sea routes. The Islamic Empire also fueled great advances in medicine, mathematics, science, and philosophy.

From ancient times, China generally had a unified empire. There were times of chaos though. For example, from 220 to 589, no ruler was strong enough to hold China together. But generally one dynasty followed another with only slight disruption, and China was diverse and prosperous. In 1234, the Mongols—invaders from the region north of China—took over China, establishing the Mongol (or Yuan) dynasty. The first Yuan emperor was Kublai Khan. China wasn't the only region ruled by the Mongols. Conquering the Islamic Empire and all of Russia as well, the Mongol Empire, which lasted until the mid-1300s, was the largest land empire in history.

The World's Longest-Lasting Empires			
Empire (region)	**Dates**	**Empire (region)**	**Dates**
Babylonian Empire (Mesopotamia)	2000 B.C.–1500 B.C.	Islamic Empire	750–1250
Hittite Empire (Mesopotamia/Asia Minor)	1650 B.C.–1200 B.C.	Khmer Empire (Southeast Asia)	802–1431
Han Dynasty (China)	202 B.C.–A.D. 220	Ottoman Empire (Eastern Europe/Turkey/the Middle East)	1361–1918
Roman Empire	44 B.C.–A.D. 476		
Byzantine Empire (Eastern Europe/Turkey)	395–1453	Russian Empire	1480–1917

Although the Islamic Empire was destroyed by the Mongols in the mid-1200s, the religion of Islam had spread throughout many parts of Africa. In western Africa, the Empire of Mali arose in 1235, around the time of the destruction of the Islamic Empire. Within a few decades, Mali became a center of Muslim learning and culture. Muslims from places as far away as Spain and western Asia went there to study.

The Toltec Empire (900 to 1200) and the Aztec Empire (1430 to 1520) were both warlike empires in the region we call Mexico today. Both empires built pyramids, temples, and palaces. Both had control over extensive trade routes. By the early 1500s, the Aztec city of Tenochtitlán was larger than any city in Europe.

Each of the empires described on these two pages eventually lost power and collapsed. Sometimes they became too large for one emperor to control. Sometimes subjects revolted against high taxes or poor rule. At other times, empires began to unravel when ethnic groups rebelled against a faraway emperor. And sometimes invaders overran an empire, creating such chaos and destruction that the empire toppled.

THEMES IN WORLD HISTORY ■ PRACTICE 2

A. **Using the chart and the information on pages 42 and 43, use letters to list the empires in order based on which was established first, second, and so on. The first one is done for you.**

1. ____ Roman Empire
4. ____ Mali Empire
7. ____ Aztec Empire

2. _a_ Babylonian Empire
5. ____ Ottoman Empire
8. ____ Byzantine Empire

3. ____ Islamic Empire
6. ____ Han Dynasty
9. ____ Greek Empire

B. **Use the information on pages 42 and 43 to answer the following question.**

10. On the lines below, list factors that led to the rise, success, and fall of empires.

Rise of empires: _____

Success of empires: _____

Fall of empires: _____

Answers and explanations start on page 132.

"One development that set the stage for modern political structures was the transition from empires to nations in Europe."

The Rise of Modern Nations

In the last years of the Roman Empire, at the beginning of the fifth century, Germanic peoples who lived along the empire's northern frontier began to invade Roman lands. The Visigoths and the Vandals attacked Rome so fiercely they all but leveled it. To some, the fall of Rome seemed like the end of the world. Europe was entering a period sometimes known as the Dark Ages, but more generally called the **Middle Ages.** The Middle Ages began in about 500; in some parts of Europe, the Middle Ages lasted until 1500.

Feudalism and the Consolidation of Royal Power

As Rome collapsed, the disappearance of a strong central government led to great disorder. Bands of criminals attacked travelers and towns, disrupting trade. The economy declined so much that people abandoned the urban areas. They moved to the country, where they could survive by farming. Over time, order was restored in Europe through the emergence of feudalism. **Feudalism** is a system of government and landholding based on mutual obligation and loyalty. The diagram shows how feudalism worked.

 A king granted land to a noble. In return, the noble paid taxes to the king and raised an army to help protect the king.   A noble granted land to a knight. In return, the knight served in the noble's army.

Knights, nobles, and kings all had peasants, called serfs, who worked on the land.

The serfs received protection and a place to live from the king, noble, or knight; they also received some of the food that they raised. In return, they paid taxes and gave their entire life's labor to the king, noble, or knight; they were bound to the land and could not leave it.

Feudalism lasted in Europe for several hundred years, from about 900 to 1200. A feudal system also was in place in Japan from 1192 to 1868, with samurai warriors taking roles similar to those of European knights. Around 1100, Europe's kings began gaining power, due mainly to an expansion of trade; towns that were independent of feudal **manors** sprang up. Townspeople paid taxes not to the nobles, but directly to the kings. In return, the kings protected and promoted trade. As towns grew, the kings' power increased. The kings raised armies and took control of large regions, which became Europe's nations.

Nations Form in Europe

A **nation** is a group of people united by shared customs, culture, and traditions, and often by a shared language or religion. A nation has a central government that inspires the loyalty of the citizenry. England's kings were the first to unite their lands as a nation. This occurred in the late 1100s. Portugal and Denmark each became unified nations in the 1100s, as well. France emerged as a nation a few centuries later. And Spain was united under a royal couple, Ferdinand and Isabella, in the late 1400s. Each of these European nations began as a **hereditary monarchy**—a nation ruled by one family in which the title of monarch is passed from one generation to the next.

However, not all European nations emerged in the late Middle Ages. For example, Italy and Germany remained fragmented, made up of small feudal states that often were at war with one another. Neither became a unified nation until the 1800s. Sweden became an independent nation in the 1500s. Switzerland and the Netherlands became their own nations by the mid-1600s. Other parts of Europe, including Austria-Hungary, the Balkan region, and Russia, remained part of vast, conglomerate empires into the 1900s.

While Europe was going through the turmoil of the Middle Ages, the Islamic Empire flourished in the Middle East. At the same time, China experienced a flowering of culture, first under the Tang dynasty (618–907) and then under the Song dynasty (960–1279). In North America, the Mississippian Mound Builders lived in bustling cities with huge earthen pyramids at their centers. Nations would not form in these regions nor in Africa for another few hundred years. But the concept of nationhood would play a powerful role in shaping world history from the Middle Ages to the present.

THEMES IN WORLD HISTORY ▪ PRACTICE 3

A. Write *true* or *false* next to each item.

_____ **1.** The Middle Ages began in Europe after the Roman Empire crumbled.

_____ **2.** Feudalism is organized around a strong central government.

_____ **3.** European kings gained wealth and power by taxing trade.

_____ **4.** Nations formed in Europe after hereditary monarchs lost power.

_____ **5.** Asia, Africa, and the Americas had nations long before Europe did.

B. Use the description below and the diagram on page 44 to help you match each Japanese term with a term from the European feudal system.

In feudal Japan, the emperor headed the country in name only. He put a powerful general called a shogun in charge. The shogun asked for loyalty from local landholders, called daimyo, who were supported by an army of samurai.

_____ **6.** samurai   _____ **7.** emperor   _____ **8.** shogun   _____ **9.** daimyo

a. king   **b.** noble   **c.** knight   **d.** serf   **e.** has no corresponding term

Answers and explanations start on page 132.

Nations Explore the Unknown

In 1405, Chinese admiral Zheng He set off from the coast of China with a fleet of 300 ships and a crew of 27,000. Besides soldiers and sailors, there were also doctors, accountants, and interpreters among the crew. The ships carried China's finest products—gold, silver, silks, scented oils, and beautiful porcelain vases. Traveling more than 3,000 miles, Zheng He visited ports throughout South and Southeast Asia. His mission was to impress peoples near and far with China's wealth and power. And he succeeded well. Because of voyages in which Zheng He's ships traveled as far as Arabia, Egypt, and the ports of east Africa, more than 16 countries sent China regular tribute payments. These payments, which a weaker country makes to a stronger one, continued for 400 years.

However, after Zheng He's seventh voyage in 1433, China stopped its long-distance voyages. Some in the government complained that the voyages were too expensive. They argued that China needed to protect its northern border from invaders more than it needed to send ships all over the world. Money was poured into strengthening and expanding China's Great Wall, and Chinese naval exploration came to an abrupt halt.

European Exploration

On the other side of the world, changes in Europe set the stage for European voyages of exploration that began in the late 1400s—almost 100 years after those of China.

Beginning just before 1100, European kings, nobles, and religious leaders organized a series of expeditions to what is today the Middle East to try to capture Jerusalem from the Muslims. These expeditions were called the **Crusades.** With the Crusades, thousands of Europeans traveled to Arab lands. They brought back spices, silks, sugar, perfumes, and many other goods from Persia, India, and China that were considered luxuries in Europe. Soon a brisk trade began between the Italians (who dominated the Mediterranean trade of Europe) and Muslim traders. Italians quickly became rich by selling Asian luxury goods to the rest of Europe.

With their newly acquired wealth, Italy's merchant class gained leisure time, which they used to pursue the arts, music, literature, and learning. This cultural awakening, which began in Italy around 1300, is called the **Renaissance.** The Renaissance soon spread to other parts of Europe. For instance, in 1419, the Renaissance spirit led Prince Henry, a son of Portugal's royal family, to open a school to further navigational sciences. Below are some of the innovations the Portuguese adopted or perfected:

- Caravels—large, sturdy ships that could travel against the wind
- Compasses—for easily determining direction (originally invented by the Chinese)
- Astrolabes and sextants—for determining latitude (adapted from the Muslims)
- Shipboard cannons—to defeat opponents at sea and on coastlands

With these innovations, the Portuguese were the first Europeans to set out on voyages of exploration. As the chart on page 47 indicates, in the late 1400s, Portuguese explorers sailed south around Africa; from there they headed east, toward Asia.

Early European Explorers			
Explorer	**Time Period**	**Nation Represented**	**Accomplishment**
Bartholomeu Dias	1487–1488	Portugal	Sailed around tip of Africa (Cape of Good Hope) and into the Indian Ocean
Christopher Columbus	1492–1504	Spain	Explored and colonized many Caribbean islands; explored the coast of Central and South America
Vasco da Gama	1497–1498	Portugal	Sailed around Africa to India
Amerigo Vespucci	1499–1504	Spain, Portugal	Explored the coast of South America and identified it as a continent
Vasco de Balboa	1510–1513	Spain	Crossed Central America to the Pacific Ocean
Ferdinand Magellan	1519–1522	Spain	Although Magellan died on the voyage, his crew members were the first to sail around the world.
Giovanni da Verrazzano	1524	France	Explored the east coast of North America from what is today North Carolina to Nova Scotia

At first, the main aim of European explorers was to establish their own direct trade routes to Asia and to end the Italian monopoly of the luxury trade. Seeing that the Portuguese were well on their way to establishing an eastern trade route, Spain sponsored Christopher Columbus in 1492 to search for a western trade route. Columbus thought he could cross the Atlantic Ocean and reach India, China, and the spice-rich Pacific islands. But Columbus's voyages did not get him to Asia. Instead, he landed on the Caribbean islands, between North and South America. Soon Spain and other European nations began **colonizing** the Americas. This colonization had a huge impact on people, not only in Europe and the Americas, but in Africa and Asia as well.

THEMES IN WORLD HISTORY ▪ PRACTICE 4

A. Based on the chart above, match each name with the correct description.

_____ **1.** Balboa
_____ **2.** Columbus
_____ **3.** da Gama
_____ **4.** Dias
_____ **5.** Magellan
_____ **6.** Verrazzano
_____ **7.** Vespucci

a. first European to reach the Caribbean islands
b. first European to sail around Africa
c. first to recognize South America as a continent
d. led an expedition to sail around the world
e. first European to reach India by a sea route
f. reached the Pacific Ocean by crossing Central America
g. explored North America's Atlantic coast

B. Use the information on pages 46 and 47 to answer the following question.

8. Compare the reasons the Chinese set out on voyages of exploration with those of Renaissance Europeans. How were they similar? How were they different?

_____

_____

_____

Answers and explanations start on page 133.

"The Industrial Revolution helped create the political, economic, and social structures that define our world today."

The Emergence of the Modern World

Soon after Europeans started colonizing the Americas, they started sending American crop plants back to Europe. Two of these crops—corn and potatoes—were especially nutritious and helped feed Europeans who might otherwise have starved. These and other improvements in agriculture caused Europe's population to surge in the 1600s and 1700s. Rapid population growth led to increased demand for many common items, including clothing. Increased demand spurred businesspeople to try to make money by producing more consumer goods. They invested in new machines, such as spinning machines and power looms, which could make goods cheaper and faster. Soon factories were constructed to house the new machines. This sudden growth in industry, which began in Great Britain in the mid-1700s, is called the **Industrial Revolution.**

Industrialization and Imperialism

Although the Industrial Revolution began in Britain, people in other places quickly figured out how to build the new machines. So within a few decades, factories were springing up across the United States and Europe. As the video points out, rapid industrialization brought dramatic changes to people's lives. Before the Industrial Revolution, most people worked at home, often on farms. After the Industrial Revolution, many people began working outside the home. They had to move to cities, where factories were located, to find work. This shift in population from rural regions to cities is called **urbanization.**

The Industrial Revolution led to other dramatic changes besides urbanization. It increased the demand for raw materials, such as cotton, wool, iron, and rubber. Most industrialized nations had to import at least some of the raw materials they needed to manufacture goods and keep their factories running. To ensure uninterrupted supplies of raw materials, they began looking for ways to control less industrialized regions of the world that were rich in these materials. This led to **imperialism**—the process by which a nation takes over a country or territory through political, economic, and/or military means. The map on page 49 shows the results of European and American imperialism.

Fierce competition arose among the industrialized nations as they carved Africa and Asia into colonies. This competition led to the rise of extreme **nationalism** among the industrialized nations in the late 1800s. Imperialism and nationalism led to the outbreak of World War I in 1914. And although most European colonies gained independence by the mid-1900s, the negative effects of imperialism still cause problems today, including:

- the dismantling of local economies
- the disappearance of native languages and cultures
- the destruction of rich ecosystems and the loss of local plant crops
- the rise of ethnic conflicts created by the artificial borders of former colonies

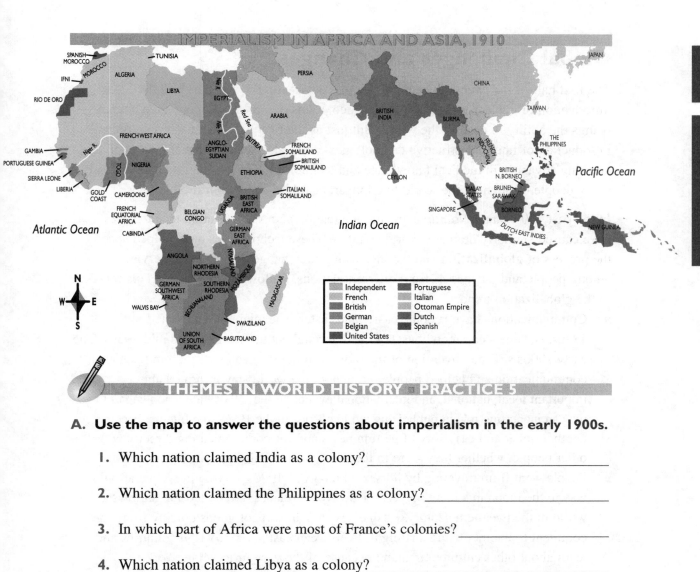

IMPERIALISM IN AFRICA AND ASIA, 1910

Legend:
- Independent
- French
- British
- German
- Belgian
- United States
- Portuguese
- Italian
- Ottoman Empire
- Dutch
- Spanish

THEMES IN WORLD HISTORY ■ PRACTICE 5

A. Use the map to answer the questions about imperialism in the early 1900s.

1. Which nation claimed India as a colony? _____

2. Which nation claimed the Philippines as a colony? _____

3. In which part of Africa were most of France's colonies? _____

4. Which nation claimed Libya as a colony? _____

5. Which nation claimed Mozambique as a colony? _____

6. Name two African countries that were not colonies but independent nations.

    _____

B. Using the information on page 48, write the letter of each phrase in the correct spot to complete the cause/effect chain below.

a. imperialism

b. a rise in demand for goods

c. feelings of extreme nationalism

d. the Industrial Revolution

e. Europe's population growth

f. World War I

g. the industrialized nations' desire to secure supplies of raw materials

7. _____ caused _____, which caused _____, which caused _____, which led to _____, which increased _____, which helped lead to _____.

Answers and explanations start on page 133.

Global Challenges and Changes

The first half of the twentieth century saw two devastating world wars and the introduction of nuclear weapons. As the video points out, these weapons give human beings the ability to destroy the world. But just as the twentieth century has seen the introduction of fatally destructive technologies, it has also seen the development of amazing advances in medical knowledge and technology. These advances have helped many people throughout the world live longer, healthier, more comfortable lives.

In the past 100 years, revolutions in communication and transportation technologies have caused similarly dramatic world changes. These technologies have helped speed the process of **globalization** and the increasing interchange of goods and services among people and businesses from different nations. Following are some details related to the globalization trend.

- Communications have become easier and faster. The telephone, invented in the 1870s, became a common household item throughout the world by the mid-1950s. The early 1900s saw the invention of the radio. It quickly became a medium for mass communication and helped people throughout the world stay informed about important local, national, and international events. In the 1950s, television began to play an increasing role in publicizing world events. In the 1990s, the Internet became another quick and easy way of getting news and for communicating directly with other people, whether they were in the next room or halfway around the world.

- People went from traveling by horse and buggy in 1900 to flying in spacecraft all the way to the moon in a mere 69 years. However, airplanes did the most to shrink the world in the twentieth century. Businesses ship all sorts of goods quickly from one continent to another using airfreight. People can easily visit foreign countries and learn about other cultures firsthand because of the vast air travel network.

- In previous centuries, the Atlantic Ocean was the main artery of world trade. Many people believe that the volume of trade in the Pacific Ocean will surpass that in the Atlantic in this century. The **Pacific Rim,** which includes the nations of East Asia, Southeast Asia, and the Americas that border the Pacific Ocean, has become a powerful force in world trade. These nations, with their large populations and well-educated workforce, are major producers and consumers of all sorts of goods. As trade increases, Asia and the Americas may draw closer culturally and economically.

Electronic components made in Taiwan (a Pacific Rim nation) are often exported to the United States.

- The rapid exchange of money and information in today's world has made countries more **interdependent** than ever before. Products made or grown halfway across the globe are a common part of people's daily lives. For example, Americans wear shoes made in Indonesia; Chinese drink American colas; and world oil prices are greatly affected by Arab nations' output.

Globalization has many benefits. It provides markets for goods and services from all nations. It provides job opportunities for people in less developed countries where jobs tend to be scarce. It also provides avenues for people from all over the world to learn more about one another and reach a deeper understanding of one another.

Globalization also has a downside. Corporations in wealthy countries can hire workers for very low wages in poorer countries; this causes a loss of jobs in the wealthier countries. In less wealthy countries, children sometimes work for pennies an hour under brutal conditions; they are deprived of educational opportunities that would help them better their lives. The exchange of cultural influences sometimes causes difficulties among peoples and societies. For example, some people object to values presented in Western movies, music, and television shows. They feel that positive elements of their culture are being overwhelmed by negative elements of Western cultures.

In the twenty-first century, people must find a way to take advantage of globalization's benefits while controlling its disadvantages.

THEMES IN WORLD HISTORY ▪ PRACTICE 6

A. Based on the information on pages 50 and 51, write the term that correctly completes each sentence.

1. _____ weapons, developed in the middle of the twentieth century, give us the capability of destroying the world.

2. Because of twentieth-century advances in _____ technologies, many people have been spared diseases and other health problems that caused early deaths in previous centuries.

3. The increasing international exchange of goods and services is one aspect of _____.

4. Radio and television have become important means of _____, which allow people to easily learn about world events as they happen.

5. The early twentieth-century invention of the _____ was the advance in transportation that has been most effective in promoting globalization.

6. The exchange of goods and services among nations of the _____ has been growing rapidly because of the region's large population and educated workforce.

B. Refer to the photograph on page 50 to answer the following question.

7. How does the photograph illustrate globalization? _____

_____

Answers and explanations start on page 133.

Apply Social Studies Information

When you **apply** social studies information, you take information you already know and use it in a new situation or context. Or you take a general principle you have learned and use it in a specific situation. On the GED Test, you may be given general information and asked to apply it to particular situations. For example, you might read a chart that describes several types of governments. Then you might be given a description of one nation's government and be asked to figure out which type it is.

When you answer **application** questions, you take general information that you've been given or that you already have and use it to answer questions about a specific situation.

EXAMPLE

Revolutions in Agriculture	
Neolithic Revolution (8000 B.C.)	People scatter wild barley and wheat seeds to grow the first crops; they tame sheep, goats, and cattle, which provide milk and meat.
Revolution in Medieval Agriculture (900)	Farmers adopt a chest harness, rather than a neck harness for horses. This allows the horse to pull a plow more efficiently, without choking. Instead of planting crops on half of their land and letting the other half lay fallow (rest), they split the land into three fields, growing wheat or rye in one field; oats, beans, or barley in the second; and letting the third lie fallow.
Enclosure Movement (1700s)	Farmers use a seed drill for planting seeds in holes at set intervals rather than scattering seeds. This boosts yields by allowing more seeds to germinate. They rotate crops on a yearly basis: one year they grow wheat, the next year a root crop, the third year barley, the fourth year clover. The crops planted in the second and fourth year help replenish the soil.
Power Revolution on the Farm (mid-1800s)	Farmers use steam-powered machines to plow and harvest crops. This allows one farmer to cultivate more land. Steam-driven transportation and refrigeration allow perishable crops to be transported to distant markets easily and quickly.
Green and Gene Revolutions (1900s)	New varieties of plant crops are produced by cross-fertilizing different strains, each with desirable traits; the resulting hybrid seeds have a higher yield. New varieties of plant crops are produced by introducing genes from other organisms directly into the seeds; the genetically-engineered seeds produce crops that are hardier or easier to harvest.

A farm family used horses to plow a single large field. They planted a different crop every year for four years in a row. Which agricultural revolution did they take part in?

a. the Neolithic Revolution   **b.** the Medieval Revolution   **c.** the Enclosure Movement

If you answered *c*, you are correct. The family's use of the four-crop rotation is the clue.

THINKING STRATEGY: In this case, you had to skim the descriptions to see which revolution included farming practices used by the family in the question.

Now let's look at some application questions similar to those on the GED Test.

Sample GED Question

A farmer plants one field of rye and a second field of oats by scattering the seeds across the ground. The farmer leaves a third field unplanted for the entire growing season.

Which agricultural revolution is the farmer a part of?

(1) the Neolithic Revolution

(2) the Medieval Revolution

(3) the Enclosure Movement

(4) the Power Revolution

(5) the Green Revolution

THINKING STRATEGY: First read the description of the farmer's method. Then skim the chart on page 52, looking for similarities between what this farmer does and the practices introduced in the different agricultural revolutions.

The correct answer is **(2) the Medieval Revolution.** The farmer divided the land into three fields; crops are planted in two of the fields, but the third field is left to lie fallow. The farmer used the sowing method of scattering seeds, which was introduced in the Neolithic Revolution and not changed until the invention of the seed drill, which was part of the Enclosure Movement. By putting this information together, you can see that this farmer was part of the revolution in medieval agriculture.

GED THINKING SKILL PRACTICE ▪ APPLICATION

The Moche people developed an impressive civilization on the coast of what is now Peru, between 100 and 700. Unlike many seacoasts, the coast of Peru is a harsh desert plain. Although the climate is very dry, rivers flow down across the desert, bringing water from the high Andes Mountains, which lie to the east. To live and farm here, the Moche built canals to irrigate their crops. They also fished the teeming waters of the Pacific, just off their coast.

Like other civilizations in the Americas, the Moche built large pyramids and palaces. They hammered gold jewelry and crafted fine clay pottery. But unusual for civilizations of the time, Moche art uses a very realistic style to show people engaged in all different activities from daily life. This art provides detailed clues about Moche culture.

Which of the following is most similar to an accomplishment of the Moche?

(1) The ancient Egyptians irrigated their fields using a type of pump called a shadoof.

(2) The Phoenicians sailed across the Mediterranean Sea and possibly explored the Atlantic coasts of Europe and Africa.

(3) The Hellenistic sculptors of Greece created realistic artwork that depicts ordinary people doing ordinary things.

(4) The Romans built aqueducts to carry water over long distances.

(5) The Venetians built their city on swampland, with canals for streets.

Answers and explanations start on page 133.

Interpret Maps

On the GED Social Studies Test, you will have to read and interpret maps. Historical maps show the relationship between geography and history. This map shows the extent of the French Empire under Napoleon Bonaparte. It also shows the route Napoleon and his army took in an attempt to conquer Russia.

EXAMPLE

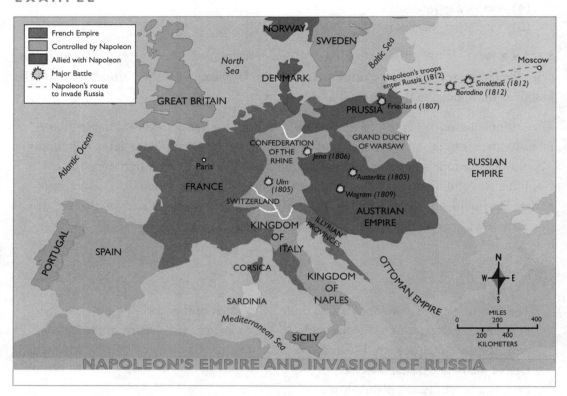

NAPOLEON'S EMPIRE AND INVASION OF RUSSIA

1. Which part of Europe was either part of the French Empire or directly controlled by Napoleon? _____

Did you say *the western part?* If so, you are right.

THINKING STRATEGY: By looking at the map key, you can see that the map shows the French Empire and countries under Napoleon's direct control in blue and purple. By looking at the compass rose, you can identify this as part of western Europe.

2. In 1810, Napoleon made an alliance with the Austrian Empire and Prussia after winning a series of battles in those regions. During what time period were those battles fought? _____

If you answered *between 1805 and 1809,* you are right. By using the map key, you can identify the symbol for major battles and locate the battles fought in Prussia and the Austrian Empire. The date of each battle is shown in parentheses after the battle's name.

Now let's look at some more map questions similar to those you will see on the GED.

GED Map Practice

Napoleon's invasion of Russia was a terrible failure. His troops took three months to reach Moscow, only to find it in flames, abandoned by the Russians. Russia's czar (emperor) refused to negotiate with Napoleon. So five weeks after entering Moscow, Napoleon retreated toward France. Of the 430,000 soldiers that began the Russian campaign, only 10,000 returned.

Based on the information above and the map on page 54, what advice might Napoleon give another military leader planning a similar invasion?

(1) Never begin an invasion right after a major military defeat.

(2) Never begin an invasion if you have to cross an ocean or a sea to attack.

(3) Never invade a country that is your ally.

(4) Never plan a land invasion across 800 miles of enemy territory.

(5) Never invade a country unless you have alliances with its neighbors.

THINKING STRATEGY: Read the choices one at a time and study the map. Remember that only one answer will agree with the information the map presents.

The correct answer is **(4) Never plan a land invasion across 800 miles of enemy territory.** Using the map scale, you can see that Napoleon's army marched about 800 miles from Prussia to Moscow. The long march across Russia caused Napoleon's defeat. The Russians torched their crops and killed their livestock, so the invading army could gather no food. Winter set in during Napoleon's retreat, and thousands of his soldiers starved or froze to death.

GED GRAPHIC SKILL PRACTICE

USING MAPS

Questions 1 and 2 refer to the map.

1. In which direction does the Nile River flow?

    (1) north   **(4)** southwest

    (2) south   **(5)** west

    (3) southeast

2. Based on the map, which technology would have aided ancient Egyptians traveling from Lower Egypt to Upper Egypt?

    (1) lighthouses, to aid safe travel along the Mediterranean coast

    (2) a canal, to aid passage around the first cataract

    (3) sails, to allow boats to travel up the Nile using the prevailing winds

    (4) horse-drawn chariots, for traveling through the Sinai

    (5) a bridge at Memphis, for crossing the Nile River

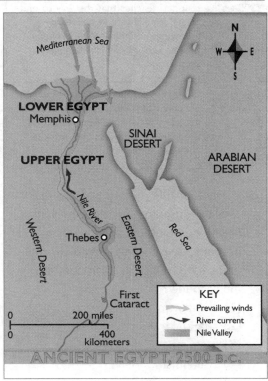

Answers and explanations start on page 133.

GED Review: World History

Choose the <u>one best answer</u> to the questions below.

Questions 1 through 4 refer to the chart below.

Some Religions of India	
Hinduism (1000 B.C./India)	No one founder; began in ancient times; teaches that the soul is reborn again and again (reincarnation) and worship of many gods, including Shiva, Vishnu, Krishna, and Rama; sacred texts include ancient texts the Vedas and the Puranas
Parsiism (600 B.C./Persia)	Zoroaster founder; Persian followers came to India around 900; teaches belief in one god (monotheism); rituals involve tending of sacred fires in Parsi temples and recitation of ancient poems
Jainism (550 B.C./India)	Vardhamana Mahavina founder; teaches that every living thing has a soul and so none should be harmed; no single sacred text; does not seek converts, so few followers outside India
Buddhism (500 B.C./India)	Siddhartha Guatana (the Buddha) founder; teaches that the way to end all suffering is to end desires, by following the Middle Way between desires and self-denial; no single sacred text
Sikhism (1400s/India)	Guru Nanak founder; combines elements of Hinduism and Islam, including belief in reincarnation and monotheism; single sacred work is the *Adi Grantha*

1. A monk of this religion wears a mask over the nose and mouth to prevent breathing in insects and carries a broom to sweep away ants or worms in his path. Which religion does the monk follow?
   (1) Hinduism
   (2) Parsiism
   (3) Jainism
   (4) Buddhism
   (5) Sikhism

2. A spiritual leader of which religion reads and interprets sacred texts that are more than 3,000 years old?
   (1) Hinduism   **(4)** Buddhism
   (2) Parsiism   **(5)** Sikhism
   (3) Jainism

3. "And what, monks, is that middle path which giveth vision? Verily, it is this . . . : Right view, right aim, right speech, right action, right living, right effort, right mindfulness, right concentration."

   Which teacher or text is this quote from?
   (1) the Vedas
   (2) Zoroaster
   (3) Vardhamana Mahavina
   (4) the Buddha
   (5) Guru Nanak

4. Which religion has its roots outside India?
   (1) Buddhism   **(4)** Parsiism
   (2) Hinduism   **(5)** Sikhism
   (3) Jainism

5. Starting around the year 800, sailors from Scandinavia called Vikings, or Norsemen, descended upon Europe, looting coastal and river towns and burning them to the ground. One Viking leader, Rollo, repeatedly attacked France. In 911, the French king granted Rollo a huge tract of land along the French coast in return for his sworn loyalty and his agreement to stop the attacks. This region came to be called Normandy, after the Norsemen.

   About how long did Europe suffer Viking attacks?
   (1) 100 years   **(4)** 900 years
   (2) 200 years   **(5)** 1,000 years
   (3) 800 years

6. Leonardo da Vinci was a genius of the Italian Renaissance. Many other artists flourished in Leonardo's Italy, but Leonardo was a true "Renaissance man"—as much a scientist as he was an artist. Leonardo's notebooks show that he imagined airplanes and submarines centuries before they became a reality. He was the first painter to dissect a human body to understand how it was put together. This understanding made him able to paint portraits of unmatched realism, and his genius gave them unmatched beauty.

What made Leonardo da Vinci a Renaissance man?

(1) He brought the Renaissance to Italy.

(2) He predicted inventions centuries before they were actually built.

(3) He was a painter.

(4) He was a scientist.

(5) He had strong interests in both the arts and the sciences.

Questions 7 and 8 refer to the map below.

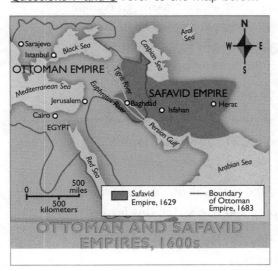

7. Which of these cities did the Ottomans and the Safavids battle each other to control between 1629 and 1683?

(1) Istanbul   **(4)** Isfahan

(2) Cairo   **(5)** Herat

(3) Baghdad

8. The Ottomans and the Safavids followed different sects of Islam. The Ottomans were Sunni Muslims; the Safavids were Shiite Muslims. The Ottomans and the Safavids battled each other for centuries.

Based on the map, which of the following is a modern-day extension of their conflict?

(1) the war Eastern Orthodox Christians fought against Sunni Muslims and Roman Catholics for control the city of Sarajevo

(2) the conflict between fundamentalist Sunni Muslims and moderate Sunni Muslims for political power in Egypt

(3) the conflict between Palestinian Arabs and Israeli Jews for control of Jerusalem

(4) the war between Sunni Iraq and Shiite Iran for control of the mouth of the Persian Gulf

(5) the conflict between Sunni Muslims in Pakistan and Hindus in India for control of territory in northern India

Question 9 refers to the photograph below.

In 1989, a rally around the "Goddess of Democracy" in Beijing shows people protesting for more freedoms.

9. What was the "Goddess of Democracy" patterned after?

(1) the Greek goddess of wisdom

(2) the German god of thunder

(3) the Italian painting *Mona Lisa*

(4) America's Statue of Liberty

(5) ancient Chinese warrior sculptures

Answers and explanations start on page 134.

Economics

LESSON GOALS

SOCIAL STUDIES SKILLS

- Learn how people make economic choices about using scarce resources
- Understand your role as a producer and consumer in the economy
- Understand the government's role in the economy

THINKING SKILL

- Analyze social studies information

GRAPHIC SKILL

- Understand graphs

GED REVIEW

1. Think About the Topic

The program you are about to watch is on *Economics*. In this program, you will learn basic information about economic choice, supply and demand, and consumer issues. About one-fifth of the GED Social Studies Test is on economics.

In this video, business people and economics teachers present important concepts. You will hear that economics is the study of the choices that individuals and societies make in using their resources. Because there are not enough resources to do everything, people must make choices about how to use their resources.

2. Prepare to Watch the Program

In this video, an economics teacher describes some thought processes that consumers use when making an economic decision. For example, she explains that when the price of pizza is high, we might decide to buy fewer pizzas per month. What might happen if the price of pizza is low?

_____

_____

You may have written something similar to: *If the price of pizza is low, we might buy more pizzas per month.*

This is an example of the law of demand. You will learn more about the laws of supply and demand in this lesson.

3. Preview the Questions

Read the questions under *Think About the Program* on the next page, and keep them in mind as you watch the program. You will review them after you watch.

4. Study the Vocabulary

Review the terms to the right. Understanding the meaning of key economics vocabulary will help you understand the video and the rest of this lesson.

WATCH THE PROGRAM

As you watch the program, pay special attention to the host. He will introduce or summarize major economics ideas that you need to learn about. The host will also provide important information about the GED Social Studies Test.

AFTER YOU WATCH

1. Think About the Program

What is a market economy?

Why is competition important in a market economy?

What is global competition?

How do you compete as a consumer in the global economy?

How do you compete as a worker in the global economy?

2. Make the Connection

In this program, you saw a financial planner and an economics teacher describing how credit cards work. They explain that using a credit card is like borrowing money unless you pay the whole balance each month. Think of your own credit card use. What are the benefits of using a credit card? What are the drawbacks?

budget—a plan for spending and saving money

consumer—an individual or organization that buys goods and services

consumer price index—a measure of the cost of goods and services bought by average households

economics—the study of how people make choices about using limited resources

goods—things that satisfy human wants and needs, like food, clothes, and houses

gross domestic product—the total value of finished goods and services produced by a nation in a year

interest—amount paid for the use of someone else's money

law of demand—economic law that shows how consumers affect price

law of supply—economic law that shows how producers affect price

market economy—an economy in which individuals make choices about what is produced and consumed

opportunity cost—what you give up when you choose to use some resources for a particular purpose

producer—an individual or organization that makes or sells a good or service

"We can't have everything, so how do we choose?"

Basic Concepts in Economics

When you shop at a mall, you see thousands of things for sale. Toys, shirts, computers, sunglasses, jewelry, video games, shoes, CDs, candles, food, books. . . . Wouldn't it be great to buy whatever you wanted? But you have only so much money. In economic terms, your wants may be limitless, but your resources are not.

What Is Economics?

As you learned in the video, **economics** is the study of how people make choices, given that their **resources** are scarce. There are several types of resources.

Resource	Description	Examples
Land	Includes land and all natural resources, even animals	Water, copper, chickens
Labor	Human work, both mental and physical	Teaching a class, building a house, driving an ambulance
Capital	Anything created by people that is used to produce goods and services	Buildings, equipment, roads, knowledge, skills
Entrepreneurship	The ability to organize and manage the land, labor, and capital required to produce goods and services	Building a company from the ground up; inventing a new product

Goods are things that satisfy human needs, such as corn, houses, computers, and socks. You can see them and feel them. **Services** are activities that satisfy needs. Dry cleaning, computer programming, and daycare are all services.

Opportunity Cost

Because our resources are scarce, using them involves trade-offs. For example, you can buy a DVD player for $200. But that means you don't have $200 to spend on clothes. You can watch DVDs all day, but that means you don't have time to go to work. When you make a choice to use resources, the **opportunity cost** of that choice is what you give up.

We calculate opportunity cost all the time, even if we don't think of it that way. We base these calculations on our knowledge and experience. We have an idea of the benefit of using our resources in a particular way. We also have an idea of the cost involved. For example, suppose you need to calculate the opportunity cost of getting a full-time job versus a part-time job. You are deciding how much of a resource—your labor—you will use. The benefit of the full-time job is that you will make more money. The cost is that you will have less time to prepare for the GED.

As you can see, opportunity cost is subjective. One person may decide a larger income is worth more than earning a GED more quickly. Another person may decide that earning a GED more quickly is worth more than earning a larger income. Each person calculates his or her own opportunity cost when making a choice about using resources.

ECONOMICS ▪ PRACTICE I

A. Use the information on pages 60 and 61 to complete these sentences.

1. Economists study how people make _____ about using their scarce resources.

2. _____ is a resource that includes a cow eating grass in a field, as well as minerals and water.

3. _____ includes things such as buildings and equipment, as well as human accomplishments such as knowledge and skill.

4. A person who starts her own business is using the resource _____ to organize and manage all her other resources.

5. When you work for someone else, you receive wages in exchange for your resource of _____.

6. What you give up when you use some of your resources on something is that thing's _____.

7. The reason that all choices involve opportunity cost is that resources are _____.

B. Use the information on pages 60 and 61 to answer the following questions.

8. What would be the opportunity cost of studying full-time for the GED Test?

_____

_____

9. Nations also calculate opportunity cost. What might people have to give up in order for a nation to use most of its resources to produce arms for the military?

_____

_____

Answers and explanations start on page 134.

Supply and Demand

Strawberries are delicious all year, but they usually cost less in July than they do in January. Similarly, a hotel room in Buffalo, New York, on average, costs less than a comparable room in New York City. Why do prices vary? They vary because of supply and demand.

The **law of demand** shows how **consumers** affect prices. It states that when the price of a good or service is higher, the quantity demanded by consumers is lower. When the price of a good or service is lower, the demand is higher. This can be shown in a line graph called a demand curve. Study the demand curve below.

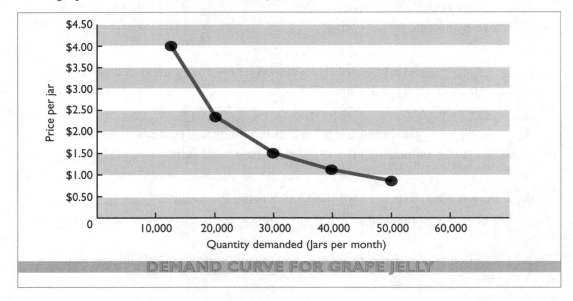

DEMAND CURVE FOR GRAPE JELLY

The **law of supply** shows how **producers** affect prices. It states that when the price is high, producers are willing to sell more of a good or service—to increase the supply. When prices are low, producers want to provide less of that good, or decrease the supply. This can be shown in a line graph called a supply curve. Study the supply curve below.

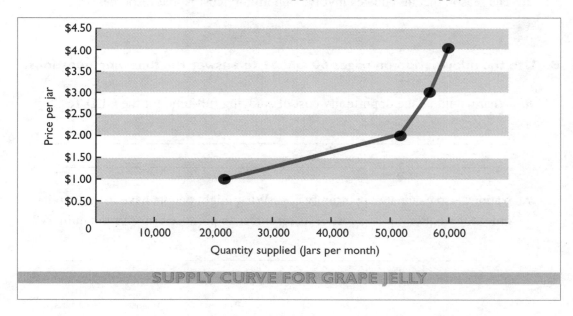

SUPPLY CURVE FOR GRAPE JELLY

The actual price of grape jelly is determined when buyers and sellers come together in the **market.** Buyers are willing to buy a certain number of jars at a particular price. Sellers are willing to supply a certain number of jars at a particular price. The price of grape jelly in that market is where the demand curve intersects, or meets, the supply curve. As you can see in the graph below, the market price for a jar of grape jelly is about $1.30.

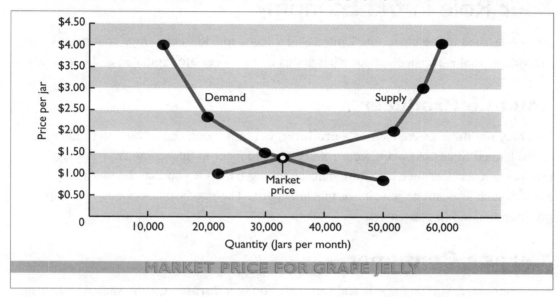

MARKET PRICE FOR GRAPE JELLY

ECONOMICS · PRACTICE 2

A. Based on the information and graphs on pages 62 and 63, write *true* or *false* next to each statement.

_____ **1.** The law of demand states that the lower the price, the higher the demand.

_____ **2.** When grape jelly costs $4 per jar, demand is approximately 10,000 jars.

_____ **3.** When grape jelly costs $4 per jar, sellers are willing to supply 20,000 jars.

_____ **4.** The lower the price of grape jelly, the more grape jelly sellers are willing to supply.

B. Use the information and graphs on pages 62 and 63 to answer the following question.

5. Because of competition, the market price is always changing. What would happen to the price of grape jelly if another seller entered the market, causing a surplus?

_____

_____

Answers and explanations start on page 134.

"In a market economy, choices are made by individuals."

Your Role in the Economy

As you learned in the video, the United States has a **market economy.** That means that individuals make decisions about what goods and services are produced and consumed.

You as a Producer

You may not think of yourself as a **producer,** but most adults contribute to production in the United States. At work, your role is as a producer in the economy. You may be producing a service, such as cutting hair or selling CDs. Or you may be producing a good, such as costume jewelry or machine parts. The goods and services you help produce are sold to consumers.

You as a Consumer

As a **consumer,** you buy goods and services. You buy **durable goods,** such as television sets and washing machines. These are goods that last a long time. You buy **nondurable goods,** such as grape jelly and detergent. These are goods that can be used up. You buy **services** such as daycare, auto repair, and plumbing repair.

In the United States, consumer spending accounts for about two-thirds of all spending for finished goods and services. Consumers have a great influence on the American economy.

Managing Your Money

As a consumer, you need to manage a scarce resource—money. You may not keep track of your spending, especially on small items. However, you are probably very aware of the big **fixed expenses** you have each month: rent or mortgage, car payments, loan payments, and so on. You are probably less aware of the **variable expenses,** such as movies, appliance repairs, and restaurant meals. These expenses change from month to month.

If you are interested in setting up a **budget** for your expenses, the best way to do this is to keep track of every penny you spend for a month. Then you can work out a budget based on your spending patterns. You can even correct any bad spending habits that you discover. The circle graph on the next page shows how the average American family of four spends money.

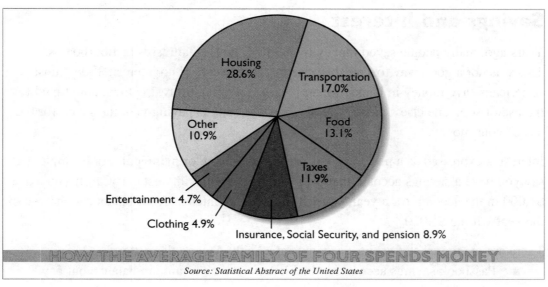

HOW THE AVERAGE FAMILY OF FOUR SPENDS MONEY

Source: Statistical Abstract of the United States

ECONOMICS · PRACTICE 3

A. Use the information on page 64 to decide whether each of the following economic activities is that of a producer or a consumer. Write *producer* or *consumer* in the space provided.

_____ **1.** Bethany takes care of kids in an after-school daycare program.

_____ **2.** Lonnie buys his wife roses every Valentine's Day.

_____ **3.** Ruthie makes beaded necklaces and earrings to sell.

_____ **4.** Matt earns extra money by shoveling snow after winter storms.

_____ **5.** Tara puts a deposit on a Caribbean cruise vacation.

_____ **6.** Darrell joins a community center and swims laps in the pool.

_____ **7.** Chandrika works as a school counselor in a high school.

_____ **8.** Ernesto hires an accountant to prepare his taxes.

B. Use the information in the circle graph above to answer these questions.

9. What percentage of the average American family's budget is spent on food?

_____

10. Compare your own family's spending with that of the average American family. In what ways is your spending similar to that of an average family? How does your spending differ from that of the average family?

_____

_____

Answers and explanations start on page 135.

Savings and Interest

Years ago, many people saved money by hiding it under mattresses or floorboards. This was not a good way to save, because the money earned no interest. Today most Americans save money in banks, where it earns interest. **Interest** is the amount paid for the use of someone else's money. In this case, the bank is paying you, the saver, for the use of your money.

Interest is expressed as a percentage of the amount saved, or **principal.** For example, let's say you have a savings account that pays 2 percent simple interest per year. If you leave $1,000 in the account for a year, you will earn $20 in interest. Your balance at the end of the year will be $1,020.

There are many types of savings accounts at a bank. Among them are:

- Passbook savings accounts, which often have no minimum balance but pay a low rate of interest.
- Certificates of deposit (CDs), which have a minimum balance and a set time period, usually from 3 months to 5 years, for the deposit. Generally, the longer the time period, the higher the interest rate. You cannot withdraw your savings until the date the CD is due without incurring a penalty.

Credit Cards and Loans

Suppose you want to buy a sofa, and you don't have enough savings to pay cash. Your wisest option would probably be to put aside money regularly in a savings account until you have enough to buy the sofa. Another option might be to use a **credit card** to finance the purchase. Using a credit card is like borrowing money. When you borrow money, you pay interest for its use. Credit card interest rates are extremely high, generally from 10 to 21 percent.

Some credit card users have trouble controlling their spending because a credit card seems like "free money." However, use of a credit card is free only if there is no annual fee for the card and you pay the balance in full each month. If you don't pay the whole balance, interest charges are applied. Interest charges can add up quickly at those high rates.

Another way to finance an essential purchase is to take out a **personal loan**. A bank or another lender advances you money for the purchase. You pay back the loan, with interest, in monthly installments. Personal loans often have high interest rates, although these rates are generally not as high as credit card rates.

When you buy a car, you can take out a **car loan.** The interest rate on a car loan is usually less than interest rates on credit cards or personal loans. That's because a car loan poses less risk to the lender. If you don't pay back the loan, the lender repossesses the car.

The bar graph on the next page shows average interest rates on three types of consumer credit.

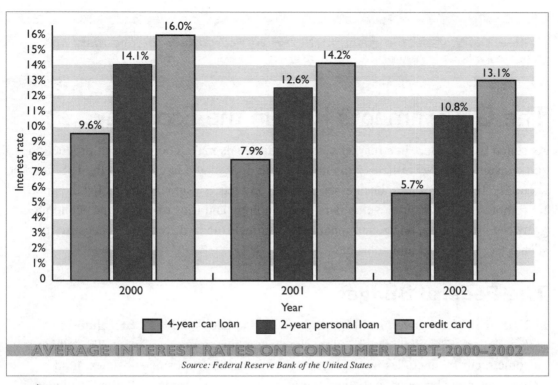

AVERAGE INTEREST RATES ON CONSUMER DEBT, 2000–2002

Source: Federal Reserve Bank of the United States

A. Based on the information on page 66, write *true* or *false* next to each statement.

_____ **1.** When you deposit money in a bank savings account, you pay interest.

_____ **2.** Interest is the amount paid for the use of someone else's money.

_____ **3.** The interest on a savings account is usually higher than that on a CD.

_____ **4.** If you pay the full balance of your credit card bill each month, you don't pay interest.

_____ **5.** A personal loan is usually paid off in monthly installments.

B. Use the information on page 66 and the graph above to answer these questions.

6. In 2000, what was the average interest rate for 4-year car loans? _____

7. In 2001, what was the average interest rate for 2-year personal loans? _____

8. In 2002, what was the average interest rate for credit card debt? _____

9. Over the three-year period shown in the graph, what trend do you see in interest rates? _____

Answers and explanations start on page 135.

"The actions of elected government officials can affect the economy and your own financial well-being in many ways."

The Government's Role in the Economy

As stated in the video, in a market system, individuals make choices about production and consumption. Nevertheless, the government does play a large role in the U.S. market economy. It regulates how businesses operate, protects consumers, and helps the poor. It promotes research and development of technology and tries to encourage economic growth. Furthermore, our government plays a direct role in the economy because it is such a large producer and consumer.

The Federal Budget

In 2001, the federal government spent about $1,856,200,000,000. That's almost *two trillion* dollars. The circle graph below shows how the money was spent. The category "income security" includes unemployment compensation, housing subsidies, food stamps, veterans' benefits, and other similar expenses. The category "other" includes such things as international affairs, science and health research, farm subsidies, federal highways, disaster relief, the courts, and administrative costs.

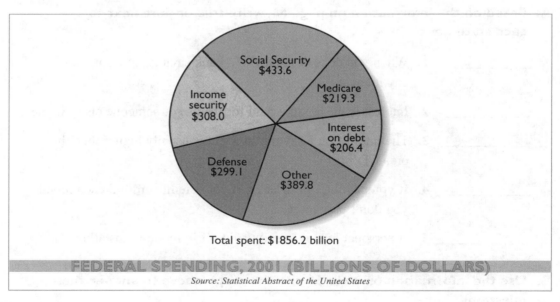

Total spent: $1856.2 billion

FEDERAL SPENDING, 2001 (BILLIONS OF DOLLARS)

Source: Statistical Abstract of the United States

Taxes

Where does the federal government get the money it spends? Most of it comes from **taxes** of various types. Three main types of taxes are listed below.

- Personal income taxes on wages, salaries, savings, and investments
- Corporate income taxes on profits made by businesses
- Excise taxes on alcohol, tobacco, telephone service, and gasoline

Sometimes the government spends more money than it receives in taxes. This is called **deficit spending.** To pay for deficit spending, the government generally must borrow money. The main way that the government borrows money is by selling bonds. You can lend money to the U.S. government by buying Series EE savings bonds, available directly from the government and from some banks. After a certain amount of time, the government pays you back, with interest. Other types of U.S. government bonds include Series I savings bonds and treasury bills. You can see from the circle graph on page 68 that paying interest on these bonds costs the government billions of dollars per year.

ECONOMICS ■ PRACTICE 5

A. Based on the information on pages 68 and 69, write *true* or *false* next to each statement.

_____ **1.** The government plays a large role in the U.S. economy by spending so much each year.

_____ **2.** The federal budget is the amount the U.S. government receives from taxpayers.

_____ **3.** The U.S. government cannot borrow money to meet its expenses.

_____ **4.** When you buy an expensive item like a car, you pay income tax on it.

_____ **5.** Businesses pay income taxes on the profits they make.

_____ **6.** It is illegal for the government to spend more money than it takes in.

_____ **7.** The U.S. government pays interest on the bonds that it sells.

B. Use the circle graph on page 68 to answer these questions.

8. In 2001, approximately what portion of federal spending was on Social Security?

_____

9. How much money did the U.S. government spend on interest payments in 2001?

_____

10. Social Security, Medicare, and income security payments are all payments to individuals for retirement, disability, health benefits, veterans' benefits, and so on. What portion of total spending do payments to individuals represent?

_____

Answers and explanations start on page 135.

Economic Statistics in the News

Many news stories about the economy are based on data the government collects. These data include the gross domestic product, the consumer price index, and the unemployment rate.

Gross Domestic Product (GDP)

Gross domestic product (GDP) is a yearly figure. The GDP represents the total value of all finished goods and services produced in the United States that year. A country's GDP is a good indicator of its overall wealth. The U.S. GDP is often mentioned in comparison with the GDPs of other nations. You can see such a comparison in the bar graph below.

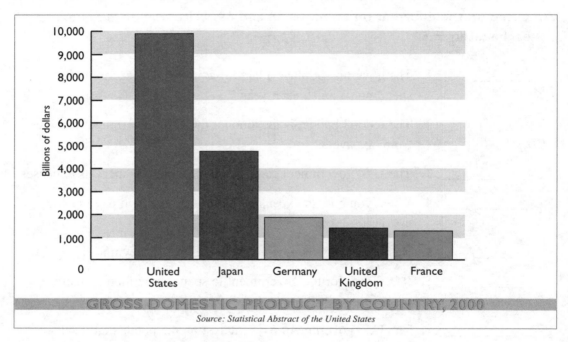

GROSS DOMESTIC PRODUCT BY COUNTRY, 2000

Source: Statistical Abstract of the United States

Consumer Price Index (CPI)

The **consumer price index** (CPI) measures the change in cost of a "market basket" of goods and services bought by the typical family. In other words, the CPI is a measure of the cost of living. Usually, the CPI goes up each year. The graph below shows recent changes in the CPI as annual percent changes.

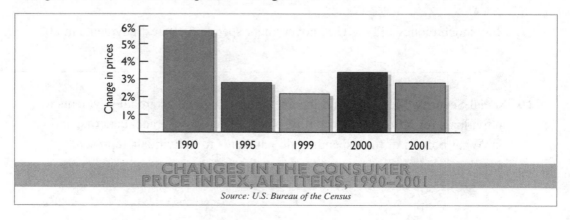

CHANGES IN THE CONSUMER
PRICE INDEX, ALL ITEMS, 1990–2001

Source: U.S. Bureau of the Census

Unemployment Rate

The **unemployment rate** is the percentage of unemployed people over age 16. It does not include people who have stopped looking for work. Generally, a high unemployment rate is a sign of poor economic times. Study the bar graph below for recent unemployment rates.

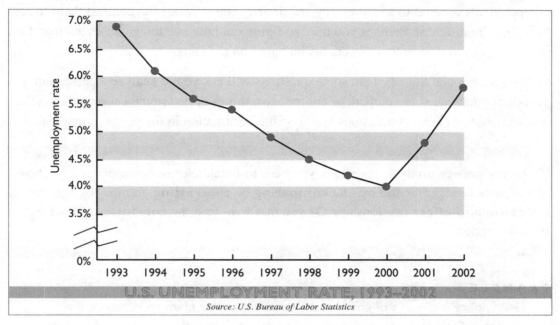

U.S. UNEMPLOYMENT RATE, 1993–2002

Source: U.S. Bureau of Labor Statistics

ECONOMICS ▪ PRACTICE 6

A. Use the information on pages 70 and 71 to complete these sentences.

1. The total value of finished goods and services produced in the United States is called the _____.

2. When the _____ goes up, people pay more for food, housing, clothing, and other items.

3. People who are looking for but cannot find work are counted in the _____.

4. Next to the United States, the nation with the largest GDP is _____.

5. The U.S. unemployment rate was lowest in the year _____.

B. On pages 70 and 71, information is provided about the GDP, CPI, and the unemployment rate. Use the information to answer the following question.

6. Which of the three economic statistics listed is most closely related to your daily life? Why?

_____

_____

Answers and explanations start on page 135.

Analyze Social Studies Information

Analysis is a thinking skill that involves breaking down information into separate parts. When you analyze information, you first find facts, ideas, and conclusions. Then you figure out the relationships among the facts, ideas, and conclusions. You may need to compare facts or ideas to see how they are similar. You may need to contrast them to see how they are different. Perhaps you need to figure out how one thing causes another. Or you may need to draw a logical conclusion based on the facts.

On the GED Social Studies Test, some questions will ask you to analyze a passage or a visual. You may need to compare or contrast two things or determine cause and effect. You may need to draw conclusions based on the information in the passage or visual.

When you answer **analysis** questions, you have to break information apart and see how all the parts fit together. You may be **comparing** or **contrasting**. You may be figuring out **cause-and-effect** relationships. Or you may have to draw **conclusions** based on the information.

EXAMPLE

Fiscal policy is the use of government spending and/or taxes to influence the economy. One of the first examples of fiscal policy in action occurred during the Great Depression of the 1930s. At the time, consumer spending and investment spending were both very low. Many people were unemployed, and demand for goods and services was low.

President Roosevelt wanted to increase demand and make the economy grow. He and Congress therefore increased government spending. As a result, demand increased in several ways. First, more government spending meant an increased demand for goods and services on the part of government. This encouraged business investment to meet that demand. In addition, both government and businesses employed more people. More people with paying jobs meant increased consumer demand.

Which of the following resulted from increased government spending in the 1930s?
a. increased demand for goods and services
b. the Great Depression

If you answered *a*, you are correct. By increasing spending, the government increased demand on the part of the government and consumers.

THINKING STRATEGY: When you look for cause-and-effect relationships, ask yourself: What caused this event or situation? What was a result of this event or situation? Sometimes words or phrases signal cause and effect. These include *caused by, because, as a result, led to, therefore,* and *as a consequence.*

Now let's look at other analysis questions similar to those you will see on the GED.

Sample GED Question

Using fiscal policy, the U.S. government influences the economy through changes in taxes and spending. Using monetary policy, the government influences the economy by making changes in the money supply. The money supply includes currency, bank deposits, and money market funds.

In the United States, monetary policy is set by the Federal Reserve Board. The "Fed," as it is called, can increase the supply of money. This stimulates the economy, or makes it grow. Or the Fed can decrease the supply of money. This slows the economy, or makes it contract.

What do fiscal and monetary policies have in common?

(1) Both directly affect the global economy.

(2) Both are ways that the government influences the economy.

(3) Both involve regulation of the money supply.

(4) Both involve changes in government spending and taxes.

(5) Both increase the amount of currency in circulation.

THINKING STRATEGY: Review the passage, looking for similarities between fiscal and monetary policy. Ask yourself, how are fiscal policy and monetary policy alike?

The correct answer is **(2) Both are ways that the government influences the economy.** The first two sentences of the first paragraph explain this.

GED THINKING SKILL PRACTICE ■ ANALYSIS

By Elena Steier. Dist. By DBR Media, Inc.

According to the cartoon, how do oil prices affect the economy?

(1) A rise in Middle East oil prices causes a rise in the price of American oil.

(2) The price of oil from the Middle East has no effect on the U.S. economy.

(3) Low oil prices slow the U.S. economy.

(4) High oil prices slow the U.S. economy.

(5) High oil prices cause economic growth in the United States.

Answers and explanations start on page 135.

GRAPHIC SKILL

Understand Graphs

On the GED Social Studies Test, you will answer questions based on one or more graphs. Graphs show numeric information in ways that help you understand it easily. Line graphs show change, often over time. Bar graphs compare and contrast different items. And circle graphs show the parts of a whole.

EXAMPLE

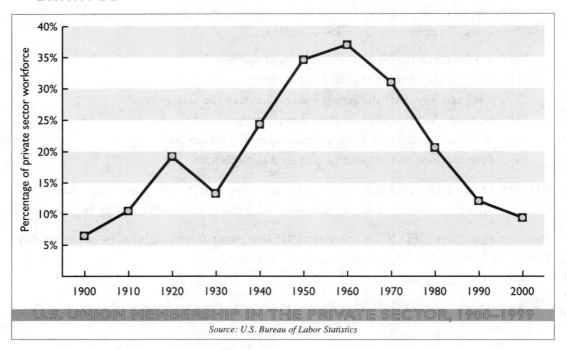

U.S. UNION MEMBERSHIP IN THE PRIVATE SECTOR, 1900–1999

Source: U.S. Bureau of Labor Statistics

1. What is the topic of this graph? _____

Did you say, *union membership in the 1900s* or *labor unions in the United States?* If so, you were right. The title tells you that the graph shows union membership among private-sector workers from 1900 to 1999. (Government workers are not included.) The title of a graph usually tells the topic of the graph.

2. Approximately what percentage of private-sector workers belonged to unions in 1920? _____

A good answer is *about 20 percent.*

THINKING STRATEGY: To find the answer, first locate the year 1920 along the bottom axis of the graph. Then scan up to locate the dot that represents the 1920 figure. Read straight across to the percentages on the vertical axis to find the correct percentage.

3. When did private-sector union membership peak? _____

The answer is *1960.* To find the peak, look for the highest point on the line graph.

Now let's look at graph questions similar to those on the GED Social Studies Test.

GED Graph Practice

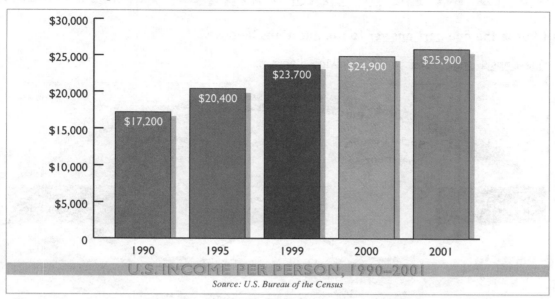

U.S. INCOME PER PERSON, 1990–2001

Source: U.S. Bureau of the Census

How much did per-person income increase from 1990 to 2001?

(1) by $3,200

(2) by $6,500

(3) by $7,700

(4) by $8,700

(5) by $9,500

THINKING STRATEGY: First locate the bar labeled 2001. The average per-person income is given as $25,900. Then find the per-person income for 1990 ($17,200). Subtract to find the difference: $25,900 – $17,200 = $8,700.

The correct answer is **(4) by $8,700.** From 1990 to 2001, average per-person income rose by $8,700.

GED GRAPHIC PRACTICE

UNDERSTANDING GRAPHS

The following question is based on the graph below.

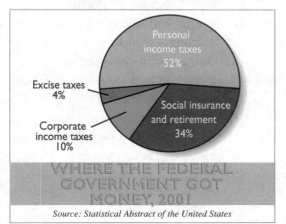

Personal income taxes 52%

Excise taxes 4%

Social insurance and retirement 34%

Corporate income taxes 10%

WHERE THE FEDERAL GOVERNMENT GOT MONEY, 2001

Source: Statistical Abstract of the United States

Approximately what fraction of federal government income comes from personal income taxes?

(1) one-half

(2) one-third

(3) one-fourth

(4) one-tenth

(5) one-twentieth

Answers and explanations start on page 135.

GED Review: Economics

Choose the <u>one best answer</u> to the questions below.

<u>Questions 1 and 2</u> refer to the following diagram.

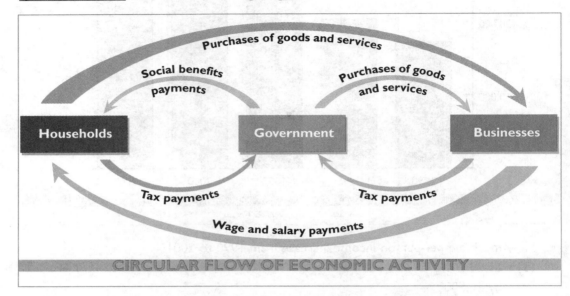

Purchases of goods and services

Social benefits payments

Purchases of goods and services

Households **Government** **Businesses**

Tax payments

Tax payments

Wage and salary payments

CIRCULAR FLOW OF ECONOMIC ACTIVITY

1. According to the diagram, what are the sources of income for households?
   (1) tax payments
   (2) purchases of goods
   (3) purchases of services
   (4) government purchases
   (5) wages, salaries, and social benefit payments

2. If households received much less than usual in income, the result would likely be
   (1) increased spending on taxes
   (2) decreased spending on goods and services
   (3) increased wages and salaries
   (4) increased economic activity by households
   (5) a halt in economic activity

3. In a command economy, major decisions about what to produce, how to produce it, and for whom to produce it are made by the central government. The government draws up a master plan, which is carried out by regional and local government agencies.

Which of the following people is most likely working in a command economy?
   (1) Joe, a government worker who plans production output for the steel factories in his area
   (2) Liz, an entrepreneur who is starting a food service business
   (3) Bill, a rancher who decides how many cattle to raise based on beef prices in the market
   (4) Sara, an employee who buys sportswear for a department store based on fashion trends
   (5) Mike, a government worker who decides to get a master's degree to change careers

Questions 4 and 5 refer to the following excerpt from the cover of a state income tax booklet.

Dear Taxpayer:

This year tight budgets will limit the number of people the Tax Division can hire to help with the upcoming tax season. This means slower processing of returns.

If you wish to get a timely income tax refund, file your return electronically ("E" file). If you cannot file electronically, make sure your preparation software puts a 2D bar code on the paper return that you file.

E-filing and 2D filing are processed very fast with very little effort. These two methods of filing will ensure that you get your refund promptly.

Sincerely,
Your Tax Administrator

4. According to the letter, why will the Tax Division have trouble processing returns quickly?
   (1) They can't accept E-filed returns.
   (2) They can't accept 2D bar code returns.
   (3) They can't accept handwritten returns.
   (4) They don't have money to hire extra help.
   (5) They don't have money to send out refunds.

5. From the information in this letter, you can conclude that refunds for taxpayers who file handwritten returns will be
   (1) processed with E-filing returns
   (2) processed with 2D bar code returns
   (3) delayed in processing
   (4) applied to next year's taxes
   (5) issued promptly

Questions 6 and 7 refer to the following circle graph.

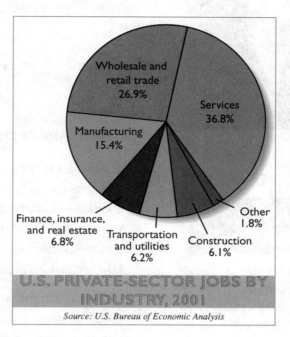

U.S. PRIVATE-SECTOR JOBS BY INDUSTRY, 2001

Source: U.S. Bureau of Economic Analysis

6. Approximately one-quarter of private-sector jobs in the United States are in
   (1) service industries
   (2) wholesale and retail trade
   (3) manufacturing
   (4) construction
   (5) transportation and utilities

7. How does the number of jobs in service industries compare with the number of jobs in construction?
   (1) Construction jobs outnumber service industry jobs two to one.
   (2) The number of construction jobs is increasing compared with the number of service industry jobs.
   (3) The number of service industry jobs and construction jobs is almost equal.
   (4) There are three times as many service-sector jobs as construction jobs.
   (5) There are six times as many service-sector jobs as construction jobs.

Answers and explanations start on page 136.

Civics and Government

LESSON GOALS

SOCIAL STUDIES SKILLS

- Learn about the structure of government and the system of checks and balances
- Understand the rights and responsibilities of citizens
- Understand how political parties, special-interest groups, and voters influence public policy

THINKING SKILL

- Analyze social studies information

GRAPHIC SKILL

- Understand editorial cartoons

GED REVIEW

1. Think About the Topic

The program you are about to watch is on *Civics and Government*. In this program, you will learn basic information about the structure of American government, the rights and responsibilities of citizens, and politics and elections. Civics and government questions make up about one-quarter of the GED Social Studies Test.

This program introduces you to the important concepts and practices in American government. These affect all of us in our daily lives, from getting a driver's license to voting.

In this program, politicians, judges, and teachers present important civics and government concepts. You will hear about the U.S. Constitution, see what it's like to vote, watch scenes from the civil rights movement, and see how hard immigrants study to become citizens.

2. Prepare to Watch the Program

In this video, you will hear about some areas of your life that are directly affected by government: getting a driver's license, buying or selling property, paying taxes. What other of your activities are affected by government?

_____

_____

You may have written something like: *obeying traffic laws, serving on a jury, buying food that meets government standards.*

3. Preview the Questions

Read the questions under *Think About the Program* on the next page, and keep them in mind as you watch the program. You will review them after you watch.

4. Study the Vocabulary

Review the terms to the right. Understanding the meaning of key civics and government vocabulary will help you understand the video and the rest of this lesson.

WATCH THE PROGRAM

As you watch the program, pay special attention to the host who introduces or summarizes major civics ideas that you need to learn about. The host will also give you important information about the GED Social Studies Test.

AFTER YOU WATCH

1. Think About the Program

Why is the U.S. Constitution so important?

What are the three branches of government?

What is the Bill of Rights?

As a voter, how can you influence what the government does?

What are some reasons why recent Hmong immigrants place a high value on becoming American citizens?

2. Make the Connection

In this program, you saw a group of volunteers helping Hmong immigrants prepare for the citizenship test. Think of a time when you did community service work. What did you do? How did your volunteer work help your community?

amendment—a change to the Constitution

Bill of Rights—the first ten amendments to the Constitution; they protect the rights of individuals

checks and balances—a system in which the branches of government have different powers, and these powers can be limited by the other branches

Constitution—the document that sets up the structure of the U.S. government

executive branch—the part of the government that carries out the laws

judicial branch—the part of the government that decides questions of law

jury—a group of citizens selected to hear evidence and decide the outcome (verdict) in a court case

legislative branch—the part of the government that makes laws

political party—a group of people who try to win elections and influence public policy

special-interest group—a group of people who share a common interest and try to influence the running of government in one or more ways

The Structure of Government

The U.S. **Constitution** is the document that set up the structure of our national, or federal, government. As you learned in the video, the people who wrote the Constitution wanted to create a strong central government. However, they were very concerned about giving too much power to one person or one section of the **federal government.** Therefore, they divided power among three branches of government: legislative, executive, and judicial.

The Legislative Branch

The **legislative branch** of government makes laws. It has the power to tax, issue money, regulate commerce, and provide for the national defense by establishing and maintaining armed forces. The legislature, called **Congress**, has two parts:

■ The **House of Representatives** consists of lawmakers elected for two-year terms. The number of representatives each state has depends on the size of its population. States with large populations have more representatives than states with small populations. Today the House of Representatives has 435 members.

■ The **Senate** consists of 100 lawmakers elected for six-year terms. Each state elects two senators, so no matter the size of the state or its population, each state has an equal number of votes in the Senate.

The Executive Branch

The **executive branch** of government enforces the law. The **president,** elected for a four-year term, is the head of the executive branch. A person can be elected president for a maximum of two terms. The executive branch also consists of many executive departments and agencies. Examples of executive departments include the Department of Education and the Department of Homeland Security.

The Judicial Branch

The **judicial branch** of government is a system of federal courts. The federal courts hear disputes related to federal laws. The **Supreme Court** is the highest court. It can settle disputes between the national and state governments and between the states. It can also declare laws unconstitutional. This means that the law goes against something in the Constitution, so the law cannot be legally carried out and is struck down.

The table on page 81 summarizes the powers of Congress, the president, and the Supreme Court.

Separation of Powers in the Federal Government		
Legislative Branch (composed of Congress)	**Executive Branch** (headed by the president)	**Judicial Branch** (headed by the Supreme Court)
• Passes laws • Passes the federal budget • Levies taxes • Regulates commerce • Issues money • Approves treaties • Approves presidential appointments	• Carries out the laws passed by Congress • Approves or vetoes (disapproves) a law passed by Congress • Appoints federal judges • Makes foreign treaties • President is commander-in-chief of the armed forces	• Can declare a law invalid because it is unconstitutional • Can settle disputes between states • Can settle disputes between a state and the national government

CIVICS AND GOVERNMENT • PRACTICE I

A. Use the information in the table above to identify the branch of government that has the power described in each item. Write *legislative*, *executive*, or *judicial* in the space provided.

_____ **1.** names judges to the federal courts

_____ **2.** decides how much to tax U.S. residents

_____ **3.** decides whether a law is constitutional

_____ **4.** issues paper bills and coins

_____ **5.** heads the armed forces

_____ **6.** settles disputes between two or more states

_____ **7.** makes treaties with foreign countries

_____ **8.** approves treaties

_____ **9.** enforces federal law

B. Use the information on pages 80 and 81 to answer the following questions.

10. Why did the people who wrote the Constitution establish three branches of government with different powers?

_____

_____

11. Franklin Delano Roosevelt served three and a half terms as president in the 1930s and 1940s. After that, the Constitution was amended, or changed, to limit presidents to two terms. Why do you think this was done?

_____

_____

Answers and explanations start on page 136.

Checks and Balances

The framers of the Constitution divided power among the legislative, executive, and judicial branches of the government. They also set up the government to make sure that each branch cannot abuse the power it has. Thus, each branch of government has the power to check the actions of the other branches. (In this context, the word *check* means "to restrain" or "to hold back.") Our government's system of power sharing is called **checks and balances.**

The diagram below shows how the president, Congress, and the Supreme Court share the power related to making and interpreting laws.

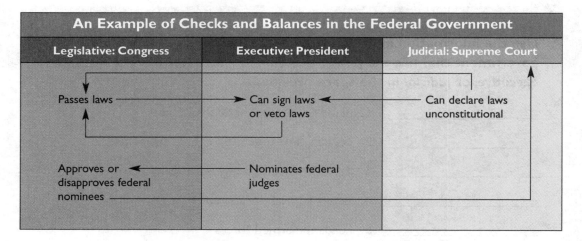

Notice how some of the checks and balances work. The president and Congress together determine who sits on the Supreme Court; the president nominates Supreme Court justices, and Congress approves or vetoes the president's nominees. Supreme Court justices can have strong influence on the government because the Supreme Court has the last say on whether a particular law is constitutional. Neither the president nor Congress can overturn decisions made by the Supreme Court. If they disagree with a Supreme Court decision, Congress must propose another law, and the process of enacting and interpreting whether the law is constitutional starts again.

Federal System of Government

The United States has a federal system of government. In a federal system, powers are divided between the federal (national) government and the state governments. The federal government can:

- Coin money
- Collect taxes, spend money, and borrow money
- Negotiate foreign treaties
- Provide armed forces for defense
- Declare war

The state governments have the power to:

- Collect taxes, spend money, and borrow money
- Set the time, place, and manner of elections
- Establish local (county, town, and city) governments
- Exert powers the Constitution does not grant the federal government and does not forbid to the states

Sometimes there is conflict between laws passed by a state and national laws. In those cases, the Constitution says that national law will be followed.

CIVICS AND GOVERNMENT ■ PRACTICE 2

A. Based on the diagram on page 82 and the information on pages 82 and 83, write *true* or *false* next to each statement.

_____ **1.** The purpose of checks and balances is to make sure that each branch of government does not abuse the power it has.

_____ **2.** The U.S. Congress nominates judges to serve on the Supreme Court.

_____ **3.** The president has more power than Congress.

_____ **4.** Congress proposes and passes laws, which the president can either sign or veto.

_____ **5.** The Supreme Court has the final word about whether a law is valid.

_____ **6.** In the United States, power is divided between national and state governments.

_____ **7.** If laws passed by Congress and laws passed by a state contradict one another, the state laws are followed.

B. Use the information about the federal system of government on pages 82 and 83 to complete the following diagram.

8.

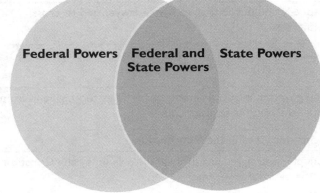

Federal Powers   Federal and State Powers   State Powers

Answers and explanations start on page 136.

"The First Amendment is our most important amendment. It gives us our five freedoms of expression."

The Rights and Responsibilities of Citizens

As you learned in the video, the Constitution was sent to the states for ratification, or approval, in 1787. Many people objected that the Constitution did not guarantee enough rights for individuals. They remembered how easily the government of England had taken away their rights before the Revolutionary War. They wanted to make sure that the new national government could not do the same thing.

The Bill of Rights

As a result of these objections, ten **amendments,** or changes, were added to the Constitution in 1791. These ten amendments are known as the **Bill of Rights.** They set forth the freedoms that the national government cannot take away from the people.

The Bill of Rights	
Amendment	**What It Provides**
First Amendment	Freedom of religion, speech, press, assembly (gathering in groups); freedom to ask the government to respond to complaints
Second Amendment	Right to bear arms (to own weapons such as guns)
Third Amendment	Prohibits the government from forcing people to house soldiers in their homes during peacetime
Fourth Amendment	Prohibits the government from unreasonably searching or seizing people and property
Fifth Amendment	Rights of people accused of a crime: they must be indicted by a grand jury in cases of major crimes; they cannot be tried twice if found not guilty; they cannot be forced to testify against themselves; due process of law must be followed
Sixth Amendment	Right to a speedy and public trial, to have a lawyer, and to cross-examine witnesses
Seventh Amendment	Right to a trial by jury in civil (noncriminal) cases if enough money is at stake
Eighth Amendment	Prohibits the government from setting bail or fines too high and from enacting cruel and unusual punishments
Ninth Amendment	Protects rights not listed in the Constitution
Tenth Amendment	States or people have rights not prohibited to them by the Constitution or given to the national government

The rights and freedoms set forth in the Bill of Rights are open to interpretation and disagreement. Even today, issues involving the Bill of Rights are at the forefront of the news. Some recent, important issues relating to the Bill of Rights include:

- Whether prayers can be said in public schools (First Amendment)
- Whether hate speech should be banned (First Amendment)
- Whether the rise in gun-related crime means that gun ownership should be limited (Second Amendment)
- Whether the death penalty is a cruel and unusual punishment (Eighth Amendment)

CIVICS AND GOVERNMENT ▪ PRACTICE 3

A. Use the information on page 84 to match each right or freedom with the appropriate amendment from the Bill of Rights. Write the letter of the amendment in the space provided. (An amendment may be used more than once.)

_____ **1.** right to bear arms

_____ **2.** right not to testify against yourself in a trial

_____ **3.** right to due process of law

_____ **4.** no cruel and unusual punishment

_____ **5.** freedom of speech

_____ **6.** no unreasonable search and seizure

_____ **7.** right to a speedy and public trial

_____ **8.** freedom of the press

_____ **9.** right to a trial with a jury in a civil case

_____ **10.** freedom of religion

_____ **11.** no unreasonably high fines or bail can be set

a. First Amendment

b. Second Amendment

c. Fourth Amendment

d. Fifth Amendment

e. Sixth Amendment

f. Seventh Amendment

g. Eighth Amendment

h. Ninth Amendment

B. Use the information on pages 84 and 85 to answer the following questions.

12. A person testifying at a trial refuses to answer a question. She says, "I take the Fifth." What right under the Fifth Amendment is that person exercising?

_____

13. The Supreme Court has held that burning the American flag is legal. They call burning the flag "symbolic speech." Which amendment protects burning the flag?

_____

14. Two police officers come to a person's house and order the person to allow them to conduct a search. They have no warrant, so the person refuses to allow them to come in. Which amendment gives the person justification for refusing the police officers' request? Explain.

_____

Answers and explanations start on page 137.

Voting

In a democracy, voting is both a right and a responsibility. All American citizens who meet certain qualifications set by law have the *right* to vote. They have the *responsibility* to participate in the political process and to vote in order to help ensure that the officials elected to the government represent their views and are responsive to their needs.

When the Constitution was first drafted, the people who wrote it couldn't agree on the qualifications for voting. They left the power to set voting requirements to the states. At that time, most states permitted only adult white male property owners to vote. Some states even had religious and tax requirements. Since then, the right to vote has become much broader, as the timeline shows. Today all citizens age 18 and over have the right to vote.

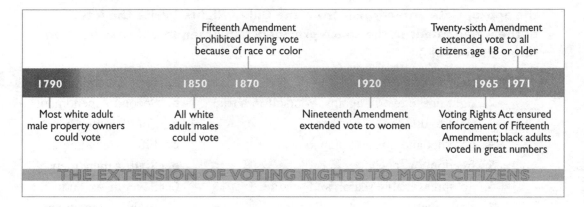

THE EXTENSION OF VOTING RIGHTS TO MORE CITIZENS

Serving on a Jury

Another responsibility of citizens is serving on a jury. A **jury** is a group of ordinary citizens who hear evidence and decide the verdict, or outcome, in a court case. There are two basic types of juries:

1. A **grand jury** decides whether a person has *probably* committed a crime. If the jury thinks the government has enough evidence to show guilt, it can charge the person with the crime. A grand jury may have up to 23 members, depending on state law. Grand juries meet in secret.

2. A **petit jury** is a trial jury. It decides whether the person on trial has broken the law. Petit juries have between 6 and 12 members. In most states, all the members of a jury must agree that a person is "guilty" or "not guilty." In other words, the verdict must be unanimous.

In most states, people who serve on juries are selected from lists of taxpayers, registered voters, or people who have obtained driver's licenses. Have you ever gotten a jury duty notice? That's an official document that orders you to appear in court as a potential juror. If you have a good reason, such as illness, you can usually postpone your jury service. Otherwise, you are put on a panel with many other potential jurors. Lawyers working on different cases then select jurors from the panel.

The Supreme Court has ruled that juries must be made up of a "fair cross section of the community." In that way, the common sense and common values of a community are applied to the practice of law. And so ordinary citizens are routinely involved in the workings of the judicial branch of government.

CIVICS AND GOVERNMENT ▪ PRACTICE 4

A. Use the timeline on page 86 to complete these sentences.

1. In the late 1700s, few people could vote because most states required that voters had to be white adult males who were _____.

2. After the Civil War, the _____ extended the right to vote to men of all races and colors.

3. Women were given the right to vote when the _____ was passed in 1920.

4. However, African Americans did not vote in great numbers until the _____ of 1965 was passed.

5. Since 1971, all citizens _____ have the right to vote.

B. Use the information on pages 86 and 87 to answer these questions.

6. Why do you think grand juries meet in secret?

   _____

   _____

7. If you were on trial for a major crime, would you prefer to be tried by a jury or to be tried by a judge alone? Why?

   _____

   _____

8. If you have ever been called for jury duty, describe the experience.

   _____

   _____

Answers and explanations start on page 137.

"I think it's incredibly important that we support candidates who have the philosophies we believe in."

Politics

In a democracy, as you may recall from the video, the people are the source of authority in government. **Politics** includes the day-to-day processes by which different groups of people pursue power and exercise it by making public policy. People have organized political parties and special-interest groups so that they can gain political power and influence public policy.

Political Parties

A **political party** is a group of people that nominates candidates to run for public office. The party chooses candidates it hopes will win elections. Members of a political party usually share a point of view on how government should work; they may also generally agree on legislation and government policies. Political parties choose candidates that support the party's views.

There are two main parties in the United States: the Democratic Party and the Republican Party. In a two-party system, each party serves as a check on the power of the other, as shown in the political cartoon below.

By Mike Lane, The Baltimore Sun.

The cartoon on page 88 was printed in newspapers around Election Day in 2002. It shows that Congress was evenly balanced between Democrats and Republicans. (In cartoons, Democrats are often represented by a donkey. Republicans are often represented by an elephant.) The cartoon shows that even one vote (for or against a congressional representative up for reelection) could ultimately alter the balance of power in Congress.

Special-Interest Groups

In addition to voting, many people also try to influence public policy by joining special-interest groups. A **special-interest group** is an organization of people linked by a motivation to further a common interest through political processes. For instance, special-interest groups try to influence who is elected and what types of laws are passed. Special-interest groups can be categorized by their common interests:

- **Economic interests**   For example, the Chamber of Commerce represents small businesses, and the AFL-CIO represents labor unions.
- **Causes or issues**   For example, the National Wildlife Federation promotes conservation, and the Campaign to Label Genetically Engineered Foods works on food labeling and other issues related to genetically engineered crops.
- **Group welfare**   For example, the NAACP promotes the interests of African Americans, and the AARP represents Americans who are 50 years old and older.
- **Public interest**   For example, the League of Women Voters encourages voters to become informed, active participants in the election process.

CIVICS AND GOVERNMENT ▪ PRACTICE 5

A. Based on the information on pages 88 and 89, write *true* or *false* next to each statement.

_____ **1.** Politics is a process by which people pursue and exercise power.

_____ **2.** In a two-party system, the parties serve to check each other's power.

_____ **3.** A political party's main goal is to have as many members as possible.

_____ **4.** A special-interest group has members with competing interests.

_____ **5.** Special-interest groups try to influence elections and legislation.

B. Use the cartoon on page 88 to answer this question.

6. After the 2002 election, the Republicans won a majority of seats in Congress. How could you redraw this cartoon to show the Republican victory?

_____

_____

Answers and explanations start on page 137.

Elections

The United States is a **representative democracy.** That means that citizens don't vote personally for every single law that is proposed. Instead, citizens elect people to represent them in local councils, state legislatures, and Congress.

Elections are therefore a very important part of the American political system. As voters, we can remove politicians who don't represent our interests. We can elect politicians who promise to do a better job. In fact, politicians are often criticized for focusing too much of their energy on getting elected, as this political cartoon shows.

Copyright © 2002 Harley Schwadron

What Happens When You Vote?

If you are a citizen over 18 and you meet your state's residency requirements, you are eligible to vote. The first step in becoming a voter is to **register.** To register, you fill in a registration form at your local board of elections, at the motor vehicles office, or wherever canvassers set up a voter registration drive. You can also register by mail. You can register as a Democrat, a Republican, or an independent with no party affiliation.

On the day of an election, voters go to their local polling place to vote. The first step is to check in with the poll workers. They have lists of voters eligible to vote in that particular voting district. As you saw in the video, you may have to show identification and sign your name. The second step is to vote. Different places use different technology. You may use a voting machine, a paper ballot, a scannable ballot, or some other form of computerized voting. Your vote is secret.

In some elections, there are referenda (plural of *referendum*) as well as candidates to vote for. A **referendum** is a proposal for a new law or for another type of public policy that is not legislated but instead put to a direct vote. Referenda may include proposals to issue bonds to raise money for building new schools; they may include proposals to abolish a tax or to change the way the tax is levied; in fact, any public issue can be the subject of a referendum.

In some elections, the list of candidates and referenda may make the ballot quite long. To help voters prepare, newspapers sometimes print a copy of the ballot ahead of time. In many states, voters receive in the mail a booklet that shows the ballot and describes the referenda before Election Day.

What happens if you will be away on Election Day? You can apply ahead of time to your local board of election for an absentee ballot. Usually you mail in the absentee ballot, and it will be opened and counted on Election Day.

CIVICS AND GOVERNMENT ▪ PRACTICE 6

A. Use the information on pages 90 and 91 to answer the following questions. Place the letter of the correct answer in the space provided.

_____ **1.** In a representative democracy, voters
  a. vote personally for each law
  b. elect people to represent them
  c. must belong to a political party
  d. always campaign for office

_____ **2.** Citizens 18 or older are eligible to vote as long as they
  a. graduated from high school
  b. belong to a party
  c. meet state residency requirements
  d. pay taxes

_____ **3.** The first step in voting is
  a. registering to vote
  b. registering with a political party
  c. going to the polls
  d. getting an absentee ballot

_____ **4.** A referendum is
  a. a type of ballot
  b. a type of voting machine
  c. a list of candidates
  d. a ballot proposal

B. Use the information on pages 90 and 91 to answer the following questions.

5. Why should voters be informed about candidates and issues before voting?

_____

_____

6. If you have voted, describe the voting technology used in your district.

_____

_____

Answers and explanations start on page 138.

Analyze Social Studies Information

When you **analyze** information, you examine it carefully. You search it for facts, conclusions, evidence, and opinions. You try to figure out the point of view of the author or artist. You "read between the lines" to discover underlying beliefs and values. You assess whether the ideas presented are valid and, if they are, whether they support a particular conclusion.

One of the key skills in analyzing social studies material is recognizing facts—information that can be proven to be true, including dates, places, statistics, and events. Another key skill is to recognize points of view, opinions, and ideas that the writer simply assumes are true.

On the GED Social Studies Test, some questions will ask you to analyze a passage or a visual. You may need to determine the author's point of view, recognize assumptions that are not actually stated, and distinguish between facts and opinions.

When you answer **analysis** questions, you have to break information apart and see how all the parts fit together. You may be determining **point of view,** recognizing **unstated assumptions,** and distinguishing **fact** from **opinion.**

EXAMPLE

> We the People of the United States, in order to form a more perfect Union, establish justice, insure domestic tranquility, provide for the common defense, promote the general welfare, and secure the blessings of liberty to ourselves and our posterity, do ordain and establish this Constitution for the United States of America.
>
> —the Preamble (introduction) to the U.S. Constitution

Which of the following did the writers of this preamble take for granted is true?
a. that people should look after personal interests before they look after community interests
b. that people have the authority to form their own government

If you answered *b,* you are correct. The framers of the Constitution believed that a government gets its powers from the people it governs.

THINKING STRATEGY: When you look for an idea that a writer takes for granted or assumes is true, you must read between the lines. Ask yourself, for this information to be true, what assumption or assumptions did the writer have to make?

Now let's look at other analysis questions similar to those you will see on the GED Social Studies Test.

Sample GED Question

Only about 50 percent of eligible voters in the United States vote in presidential elections. This is one of the lowest voter turnout rates in the world. How can voter turnout be improved in the United States? Some people believe that making voter registration easier is the key. In all states except North Dakota, citizens have to register in order to vote. In most states, they must register at least 30 days before an election. The 1993 motor-voter law makes it possible for citizens to register by mail or in motor vehicles offices, public assistance agencies, and military recruitment offices. Although more people have registered since that law passed, voter turnout has not improved substantially.

Which of the following is an opinion?

(1) About 50 percent of America's eligible voters vote in presidential elections.

(2) The United States has one of the lowest voter turnout rates in the world.

(3) Making voter registration easier will improve voter turnout.

(4) North Dakota does not require voters to be registered.

(5) The motor-voter law allows voter registration by mail.

THINKING STRATEGY: Review the passage, looking for facts (things that can be proved true). Look for opinions, both opinions of the writer and opinions of other people, mentioned in the passage. Opinions are often signaled by the words *believe* or *think*.

The correct answer is **(3) Making voter registration easier will improve voter turnout.** This opinion is signaled by the phrase *some people believe* in the fourth sentence.

GED THINKING SKILL PRACTICE • ANALYSIS

"I declined to accept the view that what was imperatively necessary for the Nation could not be done by the President unless he could find some specific authorization to do so. My belief was that it was not only his right but his duty to do anything that the needs of the Nation demanded unless such action was forbidden by the Constitution or the laws. . . . I did not usurp power, but I did greatly broaden the use of executive power."

1. Which of the following is an opinion expressed in this passage?

(1) Nations demand a lot of their leaders.

(2) America's president has many duties.

(3) A president may take any action to meet the nation's needs, if that action is legal.

(4) The Constitution can usurp the power of the president.

(5) Our government is too powerful.

2. Which of the following people most likely expressed this point of view?

(1) a strong president

(2) a weak president

(3) a vice president

(4) the Speaker of the House of Representatives

(5) the Chief Justice of the Supreme Court

Answers and explanations start on page 138.

Understand Editorial Cartoons

On the GED Social Studies Test, you will answer questions based on one or more editorial cartoons. Editorial cartoons are published in newspapers. They usually appear on the same pages as editorials, letters to the editor, and other opinion pieces. Cartoons also express an opinion—often a critical opinion—about people, events, and issues in the news. To understand an editorial cartoon, you must know something about its topic so you can understand its point of view.

EXAMPLE

THAT'S IT THEN, THE BILL OF RIGHTS IS FINISHED, BUT CAN'T WE EXCLUDE DISGUSTING RAP GROUPS AND CRAZY FLAG BURNERS?

UNFORTUNATELY, NO.

1. What is the topic of this cartoon? _____

Did you say, the *Bill of Rights* or *the First Amendment or free speech?* If so, you were right. The picture shows the framers of the U.S. Constitution. They are talking about free speech, which is protected by the First Amendment of the Bill of Rights.

2. What is the cartoonist's point of view about free speech?

_____

A good answer is, *The Bill of Rights protects all kinds of speech, even speech that some people don't like.*

THINKING STRATEGY: To find the answer, you must interpret the conversation the framers are having. One wants the First Amendment to exclude speech he finds "disgusting" and "crazy." The other tells the first man that's not possible.

Now let's look at questions about another cartoon similar to those on the GED Social Studies Test.

GED Cartoon Practice

Cartoon by John Spencer. Used with permission of the Philadelphia Business Journal.

What would be a good title for this cartoon?

(1) Two American Citizens

(2) Shopping at the Mall

(3) American Materialism

(4) Attitudes Toward Voting

(5) Voter Registration

THINKING STRATEGY: The question is asking you for the topic of the cartoon. Examine the image and the words to see what the cartoon is about.

The correct answer is **(4) Attitudes Toward Voting.** The man didn't bother to vote, and the woman thinks he was wrong not to vote.

GED SKILL PRACTICE

UNDERSTANDING EDITORIAL CARTOONS

<u>Questions 1 and 2</u> refer to the cartoon above.

1. Which view might the cartoonist support?

(1) Complain about politicians if you didn't vote.

(2) You can't change things if you don't vote.

(3) Voting doesn't give you a voice.

(4) Expressing your view on a T-shirt is important.

(5) Men and women are equally stupid.

2. What is the cartoonist most likely to say about people who don't vote?

(1) They should be forced to vote.

(2) They should run for public office.

(3) They should not be blamed for the current government.

(4) They are part of the problem.

(5) They are responsible for all of society's problems.

Answers and explanations start on page 138.

GED Review: Civics and Government

Choose the <u>one best answer</u> to the questions below.

<u>Questions 1 and 2</u> refer to the following information and diagram.

The United States and United Kingdom are representative democracies. The U.S. has a presidential government, and the U.K. has a parliamentary government.

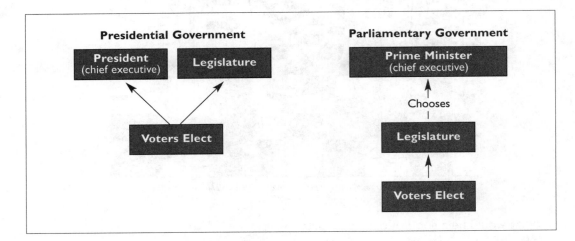

1. Who chooses the chief executive (prime minister) in a parliamentary government?
   - **(1)** judges
   - **(2)** voters
   - **(3)** the legislature
   - **(4)** the president
   - **(5)** the king or queen

2. From the diagram, what can you conclude the presidential form of government has?
   - **(1)** an appointed president
   - **(2)** an extremely powerful legislature
   - **(3)** an elected judiciary
   - **(4)** separation of powers
   - **(5)** few checks and balances

3. In 1896, the Supreme Court upheld a Louisiana law that required separate railway coaches for blacks and whites. In *Plessy* v. *Ferguson,* the Court said the law did not violate the equal protection clause of the Fourteenth Amendment because the separate railway cars for blacks were equal to those for whites.

   What do you think the Court's decision led many states to conclude?
   - **(1)** Segregating other facilities was legal.
   - **(2)** Segregation was unconstitutional.
   - **(3)** Integration was necessary under federal law.
   - **(4)** Black facilities could be substandard.
   - **(5)** White facilities could be substandard.

Questions 4 and 5 refer to the following excerpt from a juror handbook.

Some Terms You Will Hear in Court
defendant the person against whom a lawsuit is brought
plantiff the person who starts a civil case
trial juror a juror sworn in to try a particular case
deputy sheriff the officer of the court who waits on the court and the jury and maintains order in the court
court reporter the person who takes a word-for-word record of all proceedings at a trial

4. Anna fell on the snow-covered sidewalk in front of a store. She was injured, unable to work, and lost a month's pay. Anna appeared in court to sue the store.

   What role did Anna have in this courtroom?
   (1) defendant
   (2) plaintiff
   (3) trial juror
   (4) deputy sheriff
   (5) court reporter

5. After Anna recovered, she resumed her normal activities. She returned to work, where she sat in court and transcribed the proceedings of criminal cases.

   What role did Anna have in this courtroom?
   (1) defendant
   (2) plaintiff
   (3) trial juror
   (4) deputy sheriff
   (5) court reporter

Questions 6 and 7 refer to the following cartoon.

By permission of Mike Luckovich and Creators Syndicate, Inc.

6. In this cartoon, who does the man on the right represent?
   (1) a lobbyist
   (2) the Speaker of the House
   (3) a Republican
   (4) a Democrat
   (5) a member of Congress

7. With which of the following opinions would the cartoonist probably agree?
   (1) Special-interest groups play a minor role in the federal government.
   (2) Special-interest groups are essential to the legislative process.
   (3) Special-interest groups provide much-needed information to Congress.
   (4) Special-interest groups gain too much power over Congress through donations.
   (5) Members of Congress should be able to accept unlimited donations from special-interest groups.

Answers and explanations start on page 138.

Geography

LESSON GOALS

SOCIAL STUDIES SKILLS

- Learn how places are shown on maps
- Locate and describe major world regions
- Learn how people interact with their environment

THINKING SKILL

- Evaluate social studies information

GRAPHIC SKILL

- Interpret maps

GED REVIEW

1. Think About the Topic

The program you are about to watch is about *Geography*. Geography is the study of relationships between people and places. Maps are often used to convey geographical information. About 15 percent of the GED Social Studies Test is on geography.

In the video, you will learn how geographers study the physical features of regions and the cultures of peoples in different regions.

2. Prepare to Watch the Program

In this video, a geography professor describes how a British doctor used a map to help pinpoint the source of a cholera epidemic. The video also describes how two amateur geographers use a map and a GPS system to locate the intersection of a line of latitude and a line of longitude. List other possible uses of maps.

_____

_____

_____

You may have written something similar to *planning a route to drive from one place to another place*. This is an example of just one way to use a map. You probably thought of others, as well. In the video, you will see many uses for maps.

3. Preview the Questions

Read the questions under *Think About the Program* on the next page, and keep them in mind as you watch the program. You will review them after you watch.

4. Study the Vocabulary

Review the terms to the right. Understanding the meaning of key geography vocabulary will help you understand the video and the rest of this lesson.

WATCH THE PROGRAM

As you watch the program, pay special attention to the host. He will introduce or summarize major ideas about geography that you need to learn. The host will also give you important information about the GED Social Studies Test.

AFTER YOU WATCH

1. Think About the Program

What are some of the fields of study that geographers draw on?

What are physical and cultural geography?

How do people change the environment?

What are some different types of maps?

What are latitude and longitude, and how are they used?

2. Make the Connection

In this video you hear Native American Freeman Owle talk about his tribe's connection to their land. What place do you feel a special connection to? Describe the place and why it is important to you.

"Geography is a window onto the world."

The World in Maps

As you saw on the video, geographers use a wide variety of maps. In fact, we all use many types of maps. The mall directory that shows where each store is, the road map in a car's glove compartment, and the weather map shown on the evening news are all maps used in everyday life. A **map** is a visual representation of information about places, distances, and location.

The World Grid

The earliest maps were freehand drawings of land areas, bodies of water, and cities. They were not very accurate because mapmakers did not have a way to locate places precisely. To make maps more accurate, the ancient Greeks came up with a grid system similar to the one used on our maps today. The grid consists of imaginary lines of latitude and longitude.

- The red horizontal lines of **latitude** run east and west around the world. They are parallel to each other and are sometimes called parallels.
- The blue vertical lines of **longitude** run north and south between the poles. They meet at the north and south poles.

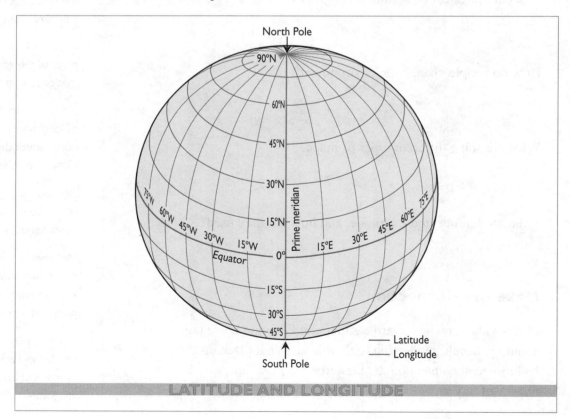

LATITUDE AND LONGITUDE

Two lines anchor Earth's grid. The first is the **equator,** the line of latitude that goes around the world halfway between the North Pole and the South Pole. The equator is 0° latitude, and the other parallels are labeled in degrees north and south of the equator. The second is the **prime meridian,** at 0° longitude. This imaginary north-south line goes through the Greenwich Observatory in London, England. The other lines of longitude are labeled in degrees east and west of the prime meridian.

The most important benefit of this grid system is that every point on Earth has a unique "address." The location of any point can be given in degrees of latitude and longitude. For example, New York City is located at 41° north latitude, 74° west longitude.

GEOGRAPHY ▪ PRACTICE 1

A. Use the information on pages 100 and 101 to complete these sentences.

1. A(n) _____ is a drawing or diagram that shows where places are located.

2. The ancient Greeks developed a(n) _____ so they could locate any place on Earth precisely.

3. Lines of _____ run east and west around the globe and are parallel to one another.

4. Lines of _____ run north and south and meet at the poles.

5. The _____ runs east and west around the world, halfway between the North Pole and the South Pole.

6. The line of 0° longitude is also called the _____.

7. To locate precisely any place on Earth, you need to give its _____ and _____.

B. The map on page 100 is divided into four main segments by the equator and the prime meridian. Match the location, given in latitude and longitude, with the map segment in which it is located.

_____ 8. 15° south latitude, 30° west longitude   **a.** upper left segment

_____ 9. 30° north latitude, 60° west longitude   **b.** upper right segment

_____ 10. 45° south latitude, 15° east longitude   **c.** lower right segment

_____ 11. 60° north latitude, 15° east longitude   **d.** lower left segment

Answers and explanations start on page 139.

Projecting the Round Earth on a Flat Map

The best type of map for showing places in their true sizes and shapes and with true distances and relative locations to one another is a **globe.** That's because Earth has three dimensions and so does a globe. However, globes are not very convenient to carry and use. Therefore, mapmakers make two-dimensional, flat **projections** of the three-dimensional Earth. In doing so, they cause distortion in their maps. How a map distorts the features it represents depends on the type of projection used for the map.

The Mercator Projection

One of the earliest projections in common use was the **Mercator projection,** named after the Flemish mapmaker who developed it in 1569. Mercator took the world grid and laid it out so that all the latitude grid lines are parallel (as they are on a globe), and all the longitude grid lines are parallel (as they are *not* on a globe). You can identify a Mercator projection by the fact that all the lines of latitude and longitude intersect at right angles.

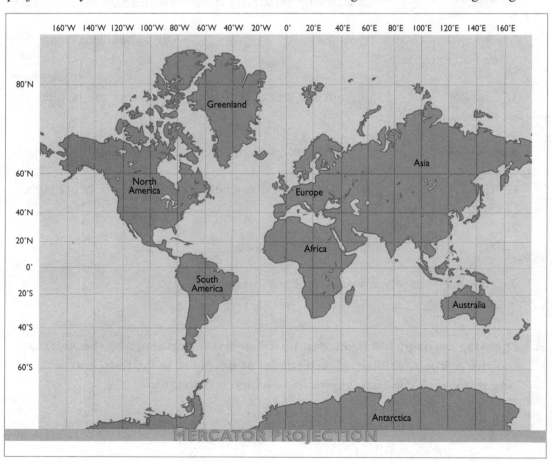

The Mercator projection distorts the shape and size of landmasses near the North Pole and the South Pole, making them look much larger than they really are. However, all directions on this map are true directions. Therefore, navigators adopted the Mercator projection because they could plot accurate courses on it. For many years the Mercator projection was the most common world map. It was popular despite its exaggeration of landmass size near the poles.

The Robinson Projection

An American, Arthur Robinson, developed a projection that decreases the distortion of lands near the poles. The advantage of the **Robinson projection** is that relative sizes of landmasses are closer to their true sizes. However, the Robinson projection does not show true direction. Still, it is a good compromise for an all-purpose map. In 1988, the National Geographic Society adopted this projection for all of its world maps.

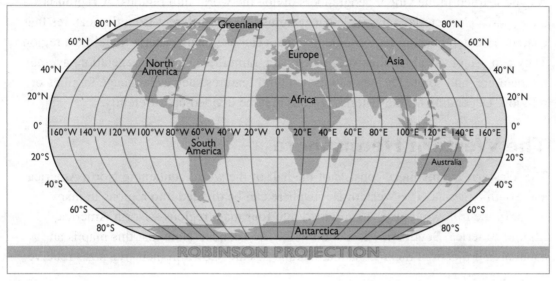

ROBINSON PROJECTION

GEOGRAPHY - PRACTICE 2

A. Based on the information and maps on pages 102 and 103, write *true* or *false* next to each statement.

_____ 1. Mapmakers use projections to turn two-dimensional maps into three-dimensional globes.

_____ 2. Different map projections distort different aspects of Earth's surface.

_____ 3. On a Mercator projection, all the lines of latitude and longitude intersect at right angles.

_____ 4. On a Robinson projection, lines of longitude get closer at the poles, so lands near the poles look closer to their true sizes.

_____ 5. Navigators used the Robinson projection because all directions on the map are true.

B. Use the maps on pages 102 and 103 to answer the following question.

6. Contrast the size of Greenland on the two maps. Why is Greenland much larger on one map than on the other?

_____

_____

Answers and explanations start on page 139.

SOCIAL STUDIES SKILLS

"A place is a location plus meaning."

World Regions

As you learned in the video, geographers divide the world into regions. A **region** is a large area characterized by particular features that are different from the features that characterize neighboring regions. Geographers can use many criteria to define a region. They can use physical features such as climate, rainfall, landscape, vegetation, average temperature, and so on. Or they can use cultural features such as language families or religion. Depending on the criteria, regions may be divided up differently.

The Western Hemisphere

The **Western Hemisphere** consists of the half of the world containing North America and South America. The Western Hemisphere can be divided into regions in many ways. In the following map, it is divided into four main regions—North America, Middle America, South America, and the Pacific Islands. (Note that this map is an equal area projection; this means that landmasses are shown in their true sizes relative to one another.)

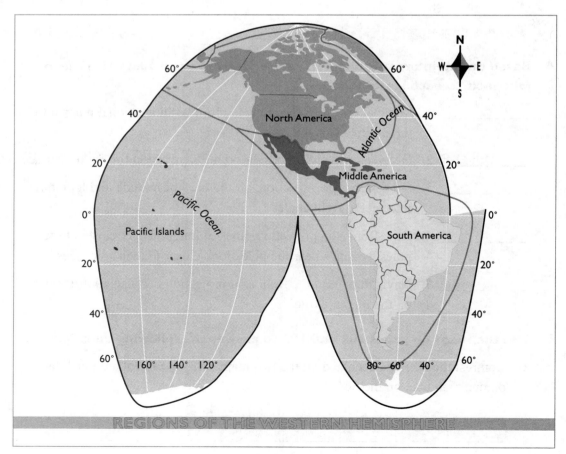

REGIONS OF THE WESTERN HEMISPHERE

The main regions of the Western Hemisphere are divided by broad physical and cultural characteristics. For example:

- North America is a **continent,** a very large landmass, inhabited mainly by peoples whose native language is English.

- Middle America consists of Mexico, Central America, and islands in the Caribbean. These places have a more tropical climate, and many of them share a common native language, Spanish.

- South America is a continent inhabited by people who generally share a common social and language background—Spanish and Portuguese.

- The Pacific Islands region consists of scattered islands inhabited by people of generally similar cultural backgrounds. A few islands in this region lie in the Eastern Hemisphere.

The boundaries between regions are not always sharp. For example, Spanish is spoken by many in the southwestern portion of North America as well as in Central America.

GEOGRAPHY ■ PRACTICE 3

A. Use the information on pages 104 and 105 to identify the correct region of the Western Hemisphere being described. Write *North America, Middle America, South America,* or *the Pacific Islands* in the space provided.

1. This region is a continent with a Latino cultural heritage. Many people descend from Spanish and Portuguese settlers, as well as from Native American inhabitants and Africans who were enslaved. _____

2. This region consists of small, widely spaced islands where people of fairly similar cultural backgrounds live. _____

3. This region is a continent where the main language is English. _____

4. This region consists of Mexico, Central America, and many small islands that share a similar climate. _____

B. Use the map and the information on pages 104 and 105 to answer these questions.

5. In which of the regions shown on the map do you live? _____

6. Many regions are smaller than the ones shown on the map. For example, the United States is divided into regions such as the Midwest, New England, and the Pacific Northwest. Which region do you live in? What are some of its characteristics? _____

_____

_____

Answers and explanations start on page 139.

The Eastern Hemisphere

The **Eastern Hemisphere** consists of the half of the world containing the continents Europe, Asia, Africa, and Australia. (Sometimes Europe and Asia are described as one continent, Eurasia.) The map below divides the Eastern Hemisphere into eight main regions—Europe, Russia, East Asia, Southeast Asia, Australia, South Asia, North Africa/Southwest Asia, and Sub-Saharan Africa. (Note that the island of New Guinea, which is part of the Pacific Islands region, is also in the Eastern Hemisphere.)

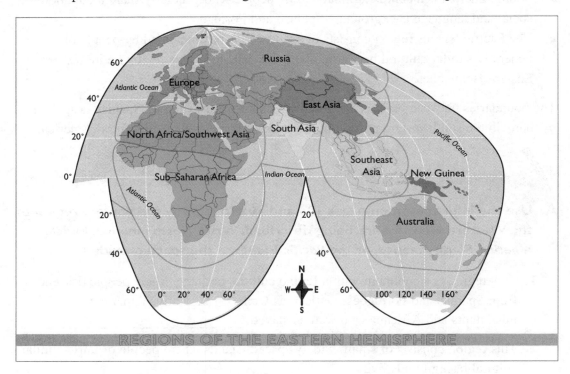

REGIONS OF THE EASTERN HEMISPHERE

Each region of the Eastern Hemisphere has distinct cultural and physical features.

- Europe is a region of small nations, many of which share a common cultural and historic tradition.
- Russia is a nation of diverse peoples who share a common historic background.
- East Asia consists of China, the Koreas, and Japan. The languages and cultures of this region share certain important similarities.
- Southeast Asia consists of many small nations such as Vietnam and Cambodia. The climate is warm, and the nations share some common cultural features.
- Australia is a continent, and New Zealand is an island nation. Both Australia and New Zealand were colonized by the British. The main language is English.
- South Asia includes India and Pakistan. Climate and historic tradition generally unite the region, while religion has sometimes caused sharp divisions.
- North Africa/Southwest Asia has a warm desert climate. Arabic is the predominant language of the region.
- Sub-Saharan Africa's climate ranges from tropical to temperate. Its natural boundary to the north is the Sahara, a large desert. This is a diverse region in terms of landscape, climate, and culture, but it is one of the world's poorest.

A. Use the information and the map on page 106 to answer the following questions. Write the letter of the correct answer in the space provided.

_____ 1. In which of the following regions is English the main language?

   a. Europe   **c.** East Asia
   b. Australia   **d.** North Africa/Southwest Asia

_____ 2. Regions close to the equator have tropical climates. Which of the following regions is most likely to have a tropical climate?

   a. Russia   **c.** Europe
   b. East Asia   **d.** Southeast Asia

_____ 3. Which region is made up of a single nation?

   a. Russia   **c.** South Asia
   b. Southeast Asia   **d.** Sub-Saharan Africa

_____ 4. Which of the following is characteristic of Sub-Saharan Africa?

   a. People speak one language.   **c.** The climate is tropical throughout.
   b. Most people are British.   **d.** The region is generally poor.

_____ 5. In which region is Arabic the main language?

   a. Southeast Asia   **c.** North Africa/Southwest Asia
   b. Australia   **d.** Europe

B. Use the information and the map on page 106 to answer these questions.

6. Many people who live in North America have ancestors who came from one of the regions of the Eastern Hemisphere. Do you have ancestors from the Eastern Hemisphere? Which region(s) did your ancestors come from?

_____

7. Which region(s) in the Eastern Hemisphere is most similar to North America in terms of culture? Why?

_____

_____

8. How do the landmasses of the Western Hemisphere, shown on the map on page 104, compare with the landmasses of the Eastern Hemisphere, shown on the map on page 106?

_____

Answers and explanations start on page 139.

SOCIAL STUDIES SKILLS

"Throughout history people have transformed their environment through the use of natural resources as well as through technology."

People and the Environment

As you saw in the video, geographers study the relationship between people and places. When people live in an area, they change it to suit their needs. They farm, they build cities and roads, and they use resources. They also adapt themselves to the places in which they live. They wear warm clothes in cold places and grow crops suited to the land and the climate.

Living in a Desert

Today, thanks to technology, many people live in places where, in the past, only a few hardy people could live. A good example is the city of Tucson, Arizona, in the American Southwest. Located in the Sonoran Desert, Tucson gets less than 12 inches of rain per year. Temperatures often climb above 100 degrees during the late spring, summer, and fall months. For years, the heat and the scarcity of water limited the number of people who lived in Tucson. In fact, until 1887, residents had to buy water for a penny a gallon from sellers who brought it to town in bags slung over the backs of donkeys.

Around 1900, the city of Tucson bought the Tucson Water Company, which piped water into town from a nearby well. As water became more available, Tucson's population grew. When air conditioning made living there comfortable, Tucson's population skyrocketed. Today about half a million people live in Tucson.

A Tucson "water cop" checks a lawn sprinkler.
People who waste water can be fined up to $1,000 per violation.

Where does Tucson's water come from today? As in the early 1900s, most of Tucson's water is piped in from wells outside the city; with a well, groundwater from deep underground is pumped to the surface. When too much groundwater is removed, the ground dries up, cracks, and sinks. Tucson also gets some water from the Colorado River, hundreds of miles from the city. The water is carried via a long aqueduct to Tucson. However, groundwater supplies are decreasing, and water from the Colorado River is expensive. Tucson relies on water use laws, conservation, reuse of wastewater, and other ways to stretch its supply of water.

GEOGRAPHY ▪ PRACTICE 5

A. Use the information on pages 108 and 109 to complete these sentences.

1. When people move into an area, they _____ to suit their needs.

2. People also _____ themselves to the places they live; for example, they wear light clothing in warm climates.

3. Tucson is located in the Sonoran Desert; it gets less than _____ inches of rain per year, and summer temperatures commonly soar above _____ degrees.

4. The invention of _____ helped boost Tucson's population.

5. Today, most of Tucson's water comes from _____; Tucson gets additional water from the distant _____.

6. Tucson tries to make the most of its water supply through _____, _____, and _____.

B. Use the photograph and the information on pages 108 and 109 to answer these questions.

7. Why is the water official concerned about the sprinkler in the photograph?

   _____

8. After the water official adjusts the sprinkler in the photograph, what other action might he take to promote water conservation?

   _____

9. List three ways to conserve water besides correctly adjusting lawn sprinklers.

   _____

10. What factors would make it difficult for people to live comfortably in an arctic environment, and how might they use technologies to live there more comfortably?

   _____

Answers and explanations start on page 140.

Natural Resources

People use resources to feed, clothe, and shelter themselves and to engage in economic activities. **Natural resources** may include air, water, land, minerals, fuels, plants, animals, and so on.

Resources and Economic Activity

The location of natural resources influences the economic activities of an area. For example, mining copper or growing bananas can't be done just anywhere; they must be done where the copper is located or where the climate and soil are suited to raising bananas.

In the United States in the late 1800s, coal was mined in the Appalachian region and iron in the upper Midwest. Both of these resources are necessary in the manufacture of steel. Both of them are also heavy and expensive to ship. Therefore, steel-manufacturing centers grew up between the coalfields and the iron mines, as shown on the map below. This location minimized the cost of shipping iron and coal to the steel factories.

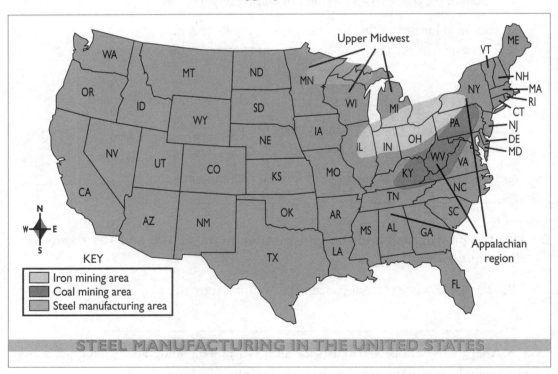

KEY
Iron mining area
Coal mining area
Steel manufacturing area

STEEL MANUFACTURING IN THE UNITED STATES

Effects of Using Resources

People need to use resources to live. But using resources can have consequences. The list below and on page 111 gives some of the negative effects of using resources:

- A growing demand for fish has caused overfishing in many ocean areas. When fishing quotas are set to allow the fish population to recover, some people involved in the fishing industry lose their livelihoods. However, if overfishing is left uncorrected, no fish would remain as food for either people or other sea creatures, and people in the fishing industry would be out of work permanently.

- In California, about 80 percent of the water goes to farms. California's cities fight among themselves and with agricultural groups for a share of the water.
- Americans burn large quantities of gasoline as they drive their cars. Burning gasoline contributes to air pollution, a particular problem in big cities with lots of cars.
- Coal is often mined by stripping off the top layer of soil and rocks to expose the coal. Then the coal is dug out. Unless the land is replanted, strip mining leaves the ground scarred and bare of soil. The burning of coal for energy also contributes to air pollution.

GEOGRAPHY ▪ PRACTICE 6

A. Use the map and the information on pages 110 and 111 to answer the following questions. Write the letter of the correct answer in the space provided.

_____ **1.** Air, water, minerals, fuels, and land are all types of
  a. places
  b. regions
  c. natural resources
  d. environments

_____ **2.** Which of the following are needed for the manufacture of steel?
  a. coal and copper
  b. land and copper
  c. land and livestock
  d. coal and iron

_____ **3.** If a region has a particular natural resource, that resource is likely to influence the region's
  a. economic activity
  b. climate
  c. latitude and longitude
  d. size

_____ **4.** When overfishing led to fishing quotas, some people who fish for a living
  a. raised fish at home
  b. lost their jobs
  c. caught more fish
  d. suddenly became wealthy

_____ **5.** What is an unintentional effect of driving cars?
  a. increased fuel supply
  b. increased life span
  c. increased air pollution
  d. decreased water supply

B. Use the information on pages 110 and 111 to answer the following questions.

6. What are some of the natural resources of the area in which you live?

_____

7. Describe one of the economic activities in your area that depends on local resources.

_____

Answers and explanations start on page 140.

Evaluate Social Studies Information

When you **evaluate** information, you judge its truth or accuracy. You assess its value. On the GED Social Studies Test, some questions will ask you to evaluate an aspect of a passage or a visual. You may need to decide whether any of the information you are given supports a conclusion. You may need to judge whether a specific bit of evidence is sufficient to support a particular conclusion. Finally, you may need to judge how values or beliefs influence human actions.

When you answer **evaluation** questions, you have to make judgments about truth, accuracy, relevance, or values and beliefs.

EXAMPLE

In some countries, people live in remote villages. They are often unwilling to be counted by the government. To do a census, some nations use spatial sampling and aerial photography. To do a spatial sample, a census taker visits a few villages, counts all the people, and figures out the average number of people per house or hut. Then photos are taken from the air of all of the distant villages. The photos are examined to see how many houses or huts there are. The number of houses or huts is multiplied by the average number of people per house or hut. The result is the estimated population of the photographed area.

1. What makes some people in remote villages unwilling to take part in their nation's census?

a. They distrust the government.   b. They prefer to count themselves.

The correct answer is *a*. Some people in remote villages believe that bad things may come from being counted. They do not want to give the government personal information, because they do not trust the government.

THINKING STRATEGY: When you look for the role that values and beliefs play in people's decisions, ask yourself: What motivates people to act this way?

2. How accurate is a count taken by spatial sampling and aerial photography?

a. completely accurate because every person is counted individually
b. somewhat accurate because the count is based on averages

If you answered *b,* you are correct. Spatial sampling and aerial photography yield a population estimate based on averages rather than a person-by-person count.

THINKING STRATEGY: When you assess the accuracy of information, examine the source of the information. Ask yourself: Are the data completely accurate? Are there any problems with the way the data were collected?

Now let's look at other evaluation questions similar to those you will see on the GED.

Sample GED Question

BOB LANG, RighToons.com

According to the cartoon, what do environmentalists believe?

(1) A hunting and gathering culture is better than a farming culture.

(2) Forests and wildlife should be used to help people make a living.

(3) Trees should be cut down by lumber companies, not by ordinary citizens.

(4) Preserving nature is more important than economic development.

(5) Limited use of natural resources is the key to happiness.

THINKING STRATEGY: Examine the cartoon. What is the cartoonist's point of view? Is he supporting or criticizing environmentalists? What values is he criticizing?

The answer is **(4) Preserving nature is more important than economic development.** According to the cartoonist, environmentalists value nature more than economic prosperity.

GED THINKING SKILL PRACTICE ■ EVALUATION

In 1798, economist Thomas Malthus noted that Great Britain's population was growing much faster than its food supply. He predicted that, in time, there would not be enough food to feed everyone in Britain.

Which of these developments supports the conclusion that Malthus was wrong?

(1) Food production has outpaced population growth in industrial nations.

(2) The population of the United States is greater than that of Great Britain.

(3) Famines continue to occur in poor nations.

(4) People in developing nations have lower average incomes than people in industrial nations.

(5) Great Britain exports wool and other goods.

Answers and explanations start on page 140.

Interpret Maps

On the GED Social Studies Test, you will answer questions based on one or more maps. Maps are visual representations of spatial information. Maps can show physical features, such as rivers and mountains; they can show features made by people, such as roads and dams. Maps can show the distribution of resources. They can also show political boundaries or historic trends. A map can show the whole world or a city block.

EXAMPLE

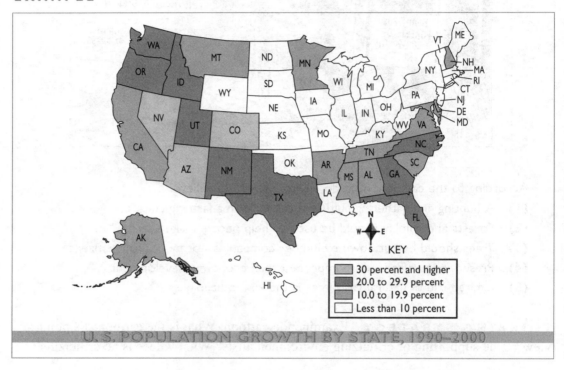

U.S. POPULATION GROWTH BY STATE, 1990–2000

KEY
- 30 percent and higher
- 20.0 to 29.9 percent
- 10.0 to 19.9 percent
- Less than 10 percent

1. What is the topic of this map? _____

Did you say: *Population growth in different states from 1990 to 2000* or *U.S. population growth by state?* If so, you were right. The title tells you that the map shows increases in state populations during the 1990s. The title of a map usually tells the topic of the map.

2. Which three states had the highest percent growth in population during the 1990s?

_____

The answer is *Nevada, Arizona*, and *Colorado*. To find the answer, first find the map key. This tells you how the ranges of percentages are represented on the map. The color orange represents the highest percentages. Look on the map to find the states shown in that color. These states had the highest percent growth in population.

Now let's look at map questions similar to those on the GED Social Studies Test.

GED Map Practice

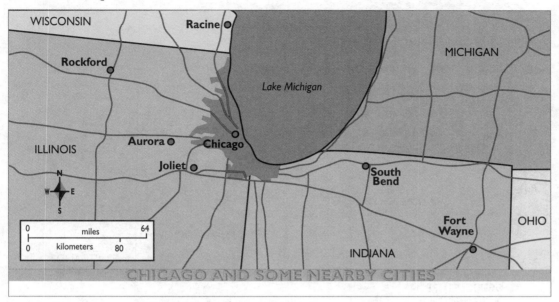

CHICAGO AND SOME NEARBY CITIES

Which of the following cities is north of Chicago?

(1) South Bend   **(4)** Aurora

(2) Fort Wayne   **(5)** Joliet

(3) Racine

THINKING STRATEGY: On most maps, north is up. However, you should check the compass rose, which is near the left edge of this map, just to make sure that north is toward the top of the map. To find the city that is north of Chicago, look for cities that appear above Chicago on the map.

The correct answer is **(3) Racine,** which is on Lake Michigan, north of Chicago.

GED GRAPHIC SKILL PRACTICE

INTERPRETING MAPS

Questions 1 and 2 are based on the map below.

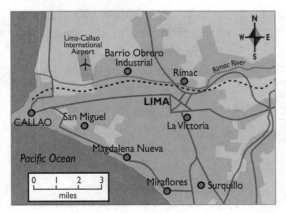

1. Which of the following suburbs is closest to the Lima-Callao International Airport?

   (1) Rimac   **(4)** Magdalena

   (2) Surquillo   Nueva

   (3) Miraflores   **(5)** San Miguel

2. Approximately how far is it from La Victoria to Magdalena Nueva?

   (1) 1 mile   **(4)** 4 miles

   (2) 2 miles   **(5)** 5 miles

   (3) 3 miles

Answers and explanations start on page 140.

GED Review: Geography

Choose the <u>one best answer</u> to the questions below.

<u>Questions 1 through 4</u> refer to the following map.

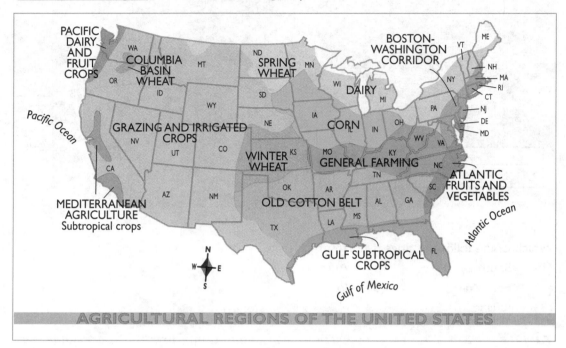

AGRICULTURAL REGIONS OF THE UNITED STATES

1. Of the regions listed, which grows the most wheat?
   - **(1)** the central United States
   - **(2)** the southeastern United States
   - **(3)** the southwestern United States
   - **(4)** the northeastern United States
   - **(5)** the northwest Pacific coastal area

2. What evidence from the map supports the generalization that the West has a dry climate?
   - **(1)** Fruit crops and dairy predominate on the Oregon and Washington coasts.
   - **(2)** Mediterranean and subtropical crops grow in parts of California.
   - **(3)** Throughout Idaho, Montana, Nevada, and Utah, crops are irrigated.
   - **(4)** Subtropical crops grow on the gulf coast of Texas.
   - **(5)** Kentucky has general farming.

3. John lives in Wisconsin, in the upper Midwest. He would like to buy a farm and earn his living by farming. John is most likely to buy a farm that produces
   - **(1)** winter wheat
   - **(2)** oranges, lemons, and grapefruit
   - **(3)** fruits and vegetables
   - **(4)** cotton and cottonseed
   - **(5)** milk and cream

4. What evidence from the map supports the conclusion that the climate of Florida is very warm?
   - **(1)** Wheat grows in the Columbia Basin.
   - **(2)** Subtropical crops grow in Florida.
   - **(3)** Florida borders the Atlantic Ocean.
   - **(4)** Many people have moved to Florida.
   - **(5)** Corn is grown north of Florida.

Question 5 refers to the following information and map.

African sleeping sickness is transmitted by the tsetse fly. The map below shows the gradual spread of the disease throughout tropical Africa.

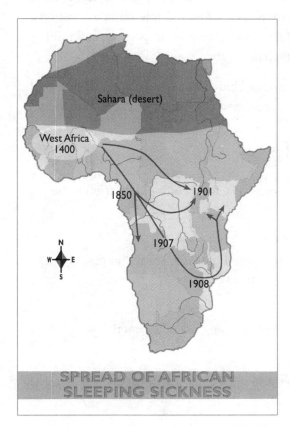

SPREAD OF AFRICAN SLEEPING SICKNESS

Question 6 refers to the following circle graph.

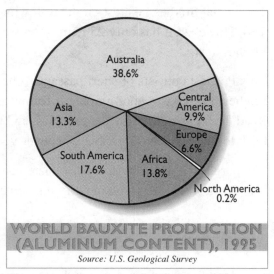

WORLD BAUXITE PRODUCTION (ALUMINUM CONTENT), 1995

Source: U.S. Geological Survey

5. Which of the following supports the conclusion that the Sahara acted as a barrier to the spread of the tsetse fly?

   (1) African sleeping sickness did not spread into North Africa.

   (2) African sleeping sickness originated in West Africa.

   (3) The first known cases of African sleeping sickness occurred around 1400.

   (4) African sleeping sickness took hundreds of years to spread southeast.

   (5) By the early 1900s, African sleeping sickness had spread into East Africa.

6. Which two regions produced about the same amount of bauxite?

   (1) Europe and North America

   (2) North America and Central America

   (3) Central America and Asia

   (4) Asia and Africa

   (5) Africa and Australia

7. A Canadian detective developed a computer program for geographic profiling. In cases involving a serial criminal, he plots locations of crime scenes and other data points involved in the crimes. Then the computer prints a map with a "hot zone," the most likely area in which the criminal lives.

   Which unstated assumption about serial criminals is the basis for this geographic profiling technique?

   (1) They are usually men under 40.

   (2) They map their crimes in advance.

   (3) They go out on crimes from a home base.

   (4) They plant false leads for detectives.

   (5) They often travel to distant countries.

Answers and explanations start on page 140.

Social Studies Posttest

The Social Studies Posttest on the following pages is similar to the GED Social Studies Test. However, it has only 25 items, compared to 50 items on the actual GED Social Studies Test.

This Posttest consists of short passages, charts, tables, diagrams, and graphs about Social Studies. Each passage or graphic is followed by one or more multiple-choice questions. Read each passage, study the graphics, and then answer the questions. You may refer back to the passage or graphic whenever you wish.

The purpose of the Posttest is to evaluate your Social Studies knowledge and thinking skills. The Posttest will help you identify the content areas and skills that you need to review.

Directions

1. Read the sample passage and test item on page 119 to become familiar with the test format.

2. Take the test on pages 120 through 127. Read each passage, study the graphics, if any, and then choose the best answer to each question.

3. Record your answers on the answer sheet below, using a No. 2 pencil.

4. Check your work against the Answers and Explanations on page 128.

5. Enter your scores in the evaluation charts on page 129.

SOCIAL STUDIES POSTTEST ◼ ANSWER SHEET

Name _____   Date _____

Class _____

1. ①②③④⑤	6. ①②③④⑤	11. ①②③④⑤	16. ①②③④⑤	21. ①②③④⑤
2. ①②③④⑤	7. ①②③④⑤	12. ①②③④⑤	17. ①②③④⑤	22. ①②③④⑤
3. ①②③④⑤	8. ①②③④⑤	13. ①②③④⑤	18. ①②③④⑤	23. ①②③④⑤
4. ①②③④⑤	9. ①②③④⑤	14. ①②③④⑤	19. ①②③④⑤	24. ①②③④⑤
5. ①②③④⑤	10. ①②③④⑤	15. ①②③④⑤	20. ①②③④⑤	25. ①②③④⑤

Sample Passage and Test Item

The following passage and test item are similar to those you will find on the Social Studies Posttest. Read the passage and the test item. Then go over the answer sheet sample and explanation of why the correct answer is correct.

Question 0 refers to the following passage.

During colonial times, farm families in the North produced most of what they needed to live. Because they made little cash, they often bartered for the goods and services they needed but that they couldn't make themselves. Some families also took in work to make extra money. In such cases, businesspeople or craftsmen supplied them with raw materials. The families then produced goods such as linens or tools. They were paid by the piece.

Between 1790 and 1830, Northern farmers began to specialize. Instead of raising everything for household use, many instead grew cash crops, which they sold for a profit. They used the income from the crops to buy the goods and services they needed.

0. According to the passage, how did farming in the North change after 1790?
    (1) Farmers grew everything they needed for their families.
    (2) Farmers began trading for the goods and services they needed.
    (3) Farmers started earning more from piecework than from farming.
    (4) Farmers began to specialize and sell cash crops for income.
    (5) Farmers left their farms and moved to the cities.

Marking the Answer Sheet

0. ①②③④⑤

The correct answer is **(4) Farmers began to specialize and sell cash crops for income.** Therefore, answer space 4 is marked on the answer sheet, as shown above. The space should be filled in completely using a No. 2 pencil. If you change your mind about an answer, erase it completely.

Answer and Explanation

(4) Farmers began to specialize and sell cash crops for income. (Comprehension) According to the second paragraph, there was a shift away from subsistence farming (growing everything a family needed) toward commercial farming (growing crops to sell for a profit) between 1790 and 1830.

Social Studies Posttest

Choose the <u>one best answer</u> to the questions below.

<u>Questions 1 through 3</u> refer to the following map.

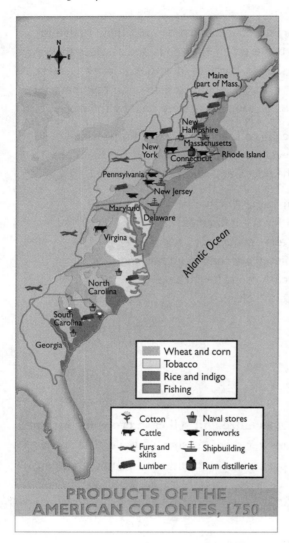

1. Lumber was one of the main products of which of the following colonies?
   (1) Maine
   (2) Connecticut
   (3) New Jersey
   (4) Maryland
   (5) Virginia

2. A shipwright from England was planning to settle in colonial America. Where would he be most likely to find work?
   (1) in Georgia
   (2) in South Carolina
   (3) in Maryland
   (4) in Maine
   (5) in Connecticut

3. According to the map, what was one of the main differences between the products of North Carolina and South Carolina?
   (1) North Carolina grew wheat and corn, and South Carolina did not.
   (2) North Carolina grew tobacco, and South Carolina did not.
   (3) North Carolina grew rice and indigo, and South Carolina did not.
   (4) North Carolina produced lumber, and South Carolina did not.
   (5) North Carolina produced naval stores, and South Carolina did not.

Questions 4 and 5 refer to the following paragraph and circle graph.

In presidential races, the Electoral College determines the winner. Each state has a certain number of votes in the Electoral College, based on the state's population. A state's Electoral College votes generally cannot be split among candidates; in most states, all of the state's Electoral College votes go to the candidate who wins the popular vote in that state. To be elected president, a candidate must win a majority of the Electoral College vote.

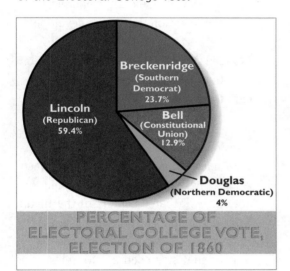

PERCENTAGE OF ELECTORAL COLLEGE VOTE, ELECTION OF 1860

4. What percentage of the Electoral College vote did Lincoln win in 1860?
   (1) 12.9%   **(4)** 39.8%
   (2) 18.1%   **(5)** 59.4%
   (3) 23.7%

5. Which fact supports the conclusion that a candidate sometimes wins very different proportions of the Electoral College vote compared with the popular vote?
   (1) Bell won 12.6% of the popular vote.
   (2) Douglas won 29.5% of the popular vote.
   (3) Breckenridge won neither the popular vote nor the Electoral College vote.
   (4) Lincoln won both the popular vote and Electoral College vote.
   (5) The Democrats split their votes between two candidates.

6. Even after the Revolutionary War began in 1775, many well-to-do, moderate colonists still hoped for a negotiated settlement with the British. They feared that independence from Great Britain would lead to chaos and threaten their financial well-being.

What did these colonists value more than independence?
   (1) stability and prosperity
   (2) liberty and equality
   (3) strength and courage
   (4) humility and self-sacrifice
   (5) rugged individualism

7. In the 1970s, the economy was stagnant, prices rose steeply, and unemployment was high. Many men who lost jobs were employed in the auto or steel industry or in other high-paying manufacturing industries. After these men lost their manufacturing jobs, their wives often took low-paying jobs in offices, shops, and restaurants. The money the women brought in helped keep their families afloat financially. In 1950, one-quarter of married women had jobs outside the home. By 1980, one-half did.

Based on the passage, why did many women enter the paid workforce in the 1970s?
   (1) to earn money before they married
   (2) to make up for the lost wages of their husbands
   (3) to gain work experience
   (4) to have a satisfying career
   (5) to learn how to manufacture cars and other products

Questions 8 and 9 refer to the following passage.

Confucius, the most influential Chinese philosopher, lived around 500 B.C., during the time of the Warring States. During this era, the Chinese emperor held little power. Instead, feudal lords vied for control of smaller territories. They fought frequent and bloody wars to try to expand their power. War was recreation for most of the nobles. The people who suffered and died in these wars were the common foot soldiers—peasants who were drafted into the nobles' armies. War was expensive, so taxes were high. Peasants had to fight rather than farm, so famine was common.

Confucius saw the turmoil and suffering. He wanted to help restore order and improve Chinese society. He proposed that society be based on reciprocal relationships. Ruler and ruled, mother and daughter, father and son would all have clear duties to one another and fulfill these duties faithfully. Then order would emerge because each person would understand the behavior required by his or her role in life.

8. Why was Confucius so concerned about maintaining social order?
   (1) He had difficulty getting along with his family.
   (2) He lived during a period of political unrest and warfare.
   (3) He had to fight the feudal lords but wanted to make peace with them.
   (4) He wanted to be able to hire more peasants to farm his land.
   (5) His society was stable and prosperous.

9. What did Confucius's system of reciprocity put a high value on?
   (1) wealth   (4) responsibility
   (2) freedom   (5) inventiveness
   (3) technology

10. After World War I, the League of Nations was formed as part of the peace settlement. The aim of the League of Nations was "to guarantee international cooperation and to achieve international peace and security."

To which of the following organizations is the League of Nations most similar?
   (1) the North Atlantic Treaty Organization, a military alliance
   (2) the European Union, an economic organization of European nations
   (3) the World Bank, an economic organization that helps developing nations
   (4) the African Union, an organization that promotes unity in Africa
   (5) the United Nations, an international peacekeeping organization

11. The Inca civilization was built high in the Andes Mountains, in valleys between ridges. These high, flat areas, called *altiplanos,* became centers of the Incan Empire. To connect their empire, the Incas built a system of roads and bridges that stretched 2,000 miles.

In 1533, the Spanish conquered the Incas. They took vast tracts of land and placed the native population in serfdom to work the mines.

Which of the following reflects the point of view of the Spanish toward the Incan Empire?
   (1) Conquerors should protect the people they conquer.
   (2) The Incan political and social order should be maintained.
   (3) The Incan Empire should be exploited for its wealth.
   (4) The Incan Empire's most valuable asset was its network of roads.
   (5) Incan civilization was superior to Spanish civilization.

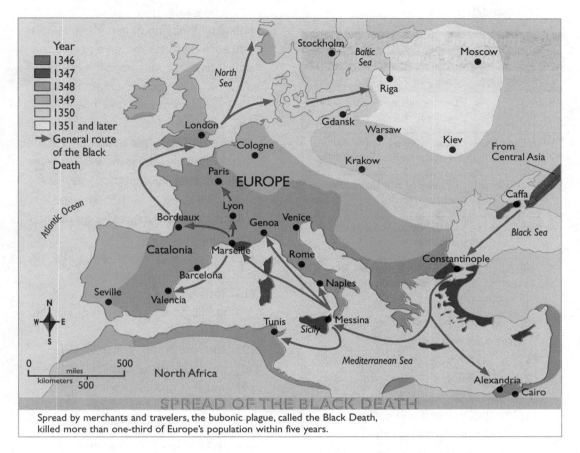

SPREAD OF THE BLACK DEATH

Spread by merchants and travelers, the bubonic plague, called the Black Death, killed more than one-third of Europe's population within five years.

12. From the island of Sicily in the Mediterranean Sea, where did the Black Death spread?

  (1) northeast to Constantinople and the Black Sea

  (2) northeast to Central Asia

  (3) southeast to Alexandria and Cairo in Africa

  (4) northwest into Europe and southwest into North Africa

  (5) northeast to Moscow and Kiev

13. From the information on the map, which of the following can you conclude?

  (1) The Black Death originated in London.

  (2) The Black Death originated in Barcelona.

  (3) The Black Death had spread through western Europe before most places in eastern Europe felt its effects.

  (4) It took more than ten years for the Black Death to reach Stockholm, Riga, and Moscow.

  (5) The Black Death affected only a small portion of Europe's population.

Questions 14 and 15 refer to the following chart.

Important Committees of the House of Representatives	
Committee	Function
Rules	Determines when a bill will be debated
Ways and Means	Deals with tax bills, Social Security, tariff and trade bills
Appropriations	Reviews all bills that authorize federal spending
Armed Services	Deals with military-related legislation.
Education and Labor	Deals with education- and labor-related bills

14. What is the function of the Appropriations Committee?

(1) to set the agenda for the House

(2) to review legislation involving federal spending

(3) to decide the qualifications for Social Security benefits

(4) to legislate matters involving labor unions

(5) to monitor the performance of the armed services

15. Representative Smith has introduced a bill that would limit imports from and exports to certain nations with poor human rights records. To which committee will Representative Smith's bill be referred?

(1) Rules

(2) Ways and Means

(3) Appropriations

(4) Armed Services

(5) Education and Labor

16. Interest groups have members with common goals. They influence public policy by lobbying public officials and influencing elections. Some people think that interest groups benefit ordinary citizens, who can participate in civic life by joining groups they favor. Others feel that interest groups raise the cost of government by pursuing policies that further narrow interests at the expense of community and national interests.

Which statement expresses an opinion about interest groups?

(1) People with shared goals join together in interest groups.

(2) Interest groups seek to shape public policy in ways that reflect their goals.

(3) Interest groups try to change policy by lobbying public officials.

(4) Interest groups may organize protests or try to influence elections.

(5) Interest groups are costly to society since they advance self-serving goals.

17. Americans are protected from unreasonable search and seizure by the Fourth Amendment. Police must get a search warrant to search homes, offices, and other places where a person could reasonably expect to have privacy. Search warrants are not required where privacy is not expected.

Which fact supports the conclusion that the police may search an open field without a search warrant?

(1) Americans are protected from unreasonable searches.

(2) The Fourth Amendment deals with searches and seizures.

(3) Places where people cannot expect privacy can be searched without a warrant.

(4) Homes and offices are considered private places.

(5) The police must get a search warrant to search a suspect's home.

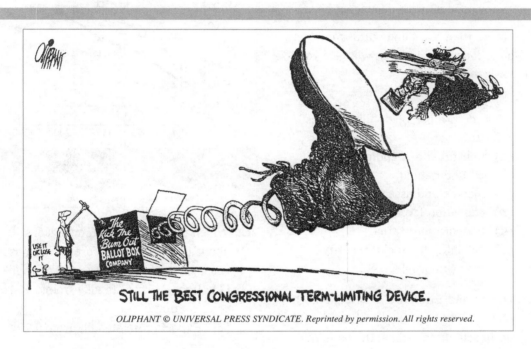

STILL THE BEST CONGRESSIONAL TERM-LIMITING DEVICE.

Questions 18 and 19 refer to the following cartoon.

18. Who is operating the "Kick the Bum Out" ballot box?

(1) a business owner

(2) a mechanic

(3) a voter

(4) the president of the United States

(5) no one; it operates automatically

19. According to the cartoonist, why is it unnecessary to limit the number of terms a member of Congress can serve?

(1) The term length for Representatives is only two years.

(2) The term length for Senators is only six years.

(3) Members of Congress can be defeated when up for reelection.

(4) Voter turnout is usually low for congressional elections.

(5) Voters can elect a new president every four years.

Questions 20 and 21 refer to the following excerpt from the Internal Revenue Service's instructions to taxpayers.

Filing Status

Check only the filing status that applies to you. The ones that will usually give you the lowest tax are listed last.

❏ Married filing separately

❏ Single

❏ Head of household

❏ Married filing jointly or qualifying widow(er) with dependent child

Tip: More than one filing status may apply to you. Choose the one that will give you the lower tax.

20. What does a person's "filing status" refer to?
(1) marital status and/or role in a household
(2) income and asset levels
(3) education level
(4) immigration status
(5) eligibility for social security payments

21. Danita and Elton are married, and they have no children. They both work and go to school part-time. Of the filing statuses they are eligible to choose, which will give them the lowest tax?
(1) married filing separately
(2) single
(3) head of household
(4) married filing jointly
(5) qualifying widow(er) with dependent child

Question 22 refers to the following information and line graph.

Imports are goods and services that the United States buys from foreign countries. Exports are goods and services that the United States sells to foreign countries. The graph shows the total value of U.S. international trade in recent years.

U.S. INTERNATIONAL TRADE, 1994–2002 (IN BILLIONS OF DOLLARS)

Source: U.S. Department of Commerce

22. Which of the following conclusions about U.S. trade with foreign nations is supported by the data on the graph?
(1) Imports rose steadily from 1994 to 2002.
(2) Exports rose steadily from 1994 to 2002.
(3) U.S. international trade peaked in 1998.
(4) The United States does very little exporting.
(5) The United States imports more than it exports.

Questions 23 and 24 refer to the following cartoon, which is set in the Arctic National Wildlife Refuge in Alaska.

Mike Keefe, The Denver Post

23. What is the main idea of this cartoon?
    (1) Oil is a good source of energy.
    (2) Animals and oil wells can coexist.
    (3) Drilling for oil in a wildlife area spoils the region for animal life.
    (4) Alternative sources of energy are no better for the environment than petroleum products.
    (5) People won't develop alternative energy sources until all oil sources are exploited.

24. According to the cartoonist, which of the following best summarizes what people in the United States value?
    (1) land in the Arctic more than land in other parts of the country
    (2) animals more than alternative energy sources
    (3) alternative energy sources more than oil
    (4) oil more than the environment
    (5) the environment more than alternative energy sources

25. People migrate to new places for many reasons. Some of the reasons are "push factors," negative characteristics of the place they live. War, political unrest, persecution, and economic hardship are all push factors. Other reasons are "pull factors." These are positive characteristics of the place the people are moving to. Peace, lack of political persecution, and economic opportunity are all pull factors.

Which of the following is a push factor that might cause people to migrate?
(1) the opportunity to start a business
(2) widespread availability of education
(3) high unemployment
(4) fertile farmland
(5) an unpolluted environment

Answers and explanations start on page 128.

Social Studies Posttest Answers and Explanations

1. **(1) Maine** (Comprehension) First find the symbol for lumber in the map's key. Maine has more lumber than any other product symbol. Therefore, lumber was one of its main products.

2. **(5) in Connecticut** (Application) A shipwright is most likely to settle in an area with a shipbuilding industry. Locate the symbol for shipbuilding in the map's key. Of the colonies listed, only Connecticut had a sizable shipbuilding industry.

3. **(2) North Carolina grew tobacco, and South Carolina did not.** (Analysis) Use the map and key to compare the products and crops that North and South Carolina produced. You can see that North Carolina has an area of tobacco, and South Carolina does not.

4. **(5) 59.4%** (Comprehension) Find the portion of the circle graph labeled "Lincoln." It indicates that Lincoln won 59.4% of the Electoral College vote. Thus, Lincoln won the presidency in 1860.

5. **(2) Douglas won 29.5% of the popular vote.** (Evaluation) Douglas won only 4% of the Electoral College vote. This is much smaller than his percentage of the popular vote.

6. **(1) stability and prosperity** (Evaluation) As the paragraph states, these colonists feared chaos, implying that they valued stability. They also feared that the war would threaten their financial well-being, indicating that they valued their own prosperity.

7. **(2) to make up for the lost wages of their husbands** (Analysis) With the decrease of manufacturing jobs, many men were out of work. Therefore, many women went to work, mostly in lower-paying service jobs, to make money for their family.

8. **(2) He lived during a period of political unrest and warfare.** (Analysis) The unsettled conditions of Chinese society concerned Confucius and led him to focus on principles that would help restore social order.

9. **(4) responsibility** (Evaluation) Confucius's system of reciprocity was based on people's responsibilities toward one another in their family and in society.

10. **(5) the United Nations, an international peace-keeping organization** (Application) The League of Nations and the United Nations are both organizations with a mission of promoting international peace. Note that the UN replaced the League of Nations after World War II.

11. **(3) The Incan Empire should be exploited for its wealth.** (Analysis) From the Spanish point of view, the value of the empire was in the economic benefits they could gain from the land and from mining.

12. **(4) northwest into Europe and southwest into North Africa** (Comprehension) The arrows show the spread of the Black Death northwest from Sicily to cities in Italy and to Marseilles in France. Another arrow points southwest to Tunis in North Africa.

13. **(3) The Black Death had spread through western Europe before most places in eastern Europe felt its effects.** (Analysis) The map shows that the Black Death spread throughout western Europe within two years. It took another year before the Black Death reached Gdansk, and at least another year before it reached other places in eastern Europe.

14. **(2) to review legislation involving federal spending** (Comprehension) In the first column of the chart, locate the Appropriations Committee. Read across the row. The chart indicates that the Appropriations Committee regulates federal spending.

15. **(2) Ways and Means** (Application) The proposed bill involves trade limits with foreign countries that have human rights abuses. Skim the "Function" column to find the committee that oversees trade-related legislation.

16. **(5) Interest groups are costly to society since they advance self-serving goals.** (Analysis) Two opinions about interest groups are stated. One opinion is against them because they try to further their own selfish interests and society winds up paying.

17. **(3) Places where people cannot expect privacy can be searched without a warrant.** (Evaluation) An open field is an example of a place where people can't reasonably expect to have privacy.

18. **(3) a voter** (Comprehension) You can infer that the man is a voter casting a ballot and affecting election results.

19. **(3) Members of Congress can be defeated when up for reelection.** (Analysis) The man getting the boot is a congressional representative. The picture and the caption imply that voting is the most effective way to limit the number of terms a member of Congress serves.

20. **(1) marital status and/or role in a household** (Comprehension) The filing status of a taxpayer is affected by marriage, divorce, death, and who else lives in a household.

21. **(4) married filing jointly** (Application) They can choose either "married filing separately" or "married filing jointly." The instructions indicate that the statuses that generally give the lower tax appear lower on the list. Since "married filing jointly" appears below "married filing separately," Danita and Elton should choose "married filing jointly."

22. **(5) The United States imports more than it exports.** (Evaluation) During all of the years shown on the graph, imports exceeded exports.

23. **(5) People won't develop alternative energy sources until all oil sources are exploited.** (Comprehension) The main idea of the cartoon can be inferred from the moose and the bear observing the oil wells and remarking that until oil runs out, people won't look for alternatives.

24. **(4) oil more than the environment** (Evaluation) The animals shown, the moose and the bear, are native to the arctic region. From the cartoonist's portrayal of the oil field and the animals' despairing tone, you can infer that the cartoonist thinks that people in the United States value oil more than they do the environment, and that the cartoonist is critical of these values.

25. **(3) high unemployment** (Application) Of the choices, only high unemployment is a negative factor that might motivate someone to leave.

Evaluation Charts for Social Studies Posttest

Follow these steps for the most effective use of the Subject Areas and Thinking Skills chart:

- Check your answers against the Answers and Explanations on page 128.
- Use the following charts to circle the questions you answered correctly.
- Total your correct answers in each row (across) for Social Studies subject areas and each column (down) for thinking skills.

You can use the results to determine which subjects you need to focus on.

- The column on the left of the table indicates the KET Pre-GED video program and its corresponding lesson in this workbook.
- The column headings—*Comprehension, Application, Analysis,* and *Evaluation*—refer to the type of thinking skills needed to answer the questions.

SUBJECT AREAS AND THINKING SKILLS

Program	Comprehension (pp. 32–33)	Application (pp. 52–53)	Analysis (pp. 72–73, 92–93)	Evaluation (pp. 112–113)	Total for Subjects
11 U.S. History (pp. 18–37)	1, 4	2	3	5, 6	___/6
12 World History (pp. 38–57)	12	10	8, 13	9	___/5
13 Economics (pp. 58–77)	20	21	7	22	___/4
14 Civics and Government (pp. 78–97)	14, 18	15	16, 19	17	___/6
15 Geography (pp. 58–77)	23	25	11	24	___/4
Total for Skills	___/7	___/5	___/7	___/6	

Many of the questions on the GED Social Studies Test are based on charts, timelines, maps, graphs, and editorial cartoons.

- Use the chart below to circle the graphics-based questions that you answered correctly.
- Identify your strengths and weaknesses in interpreting graphics by counting the number of questions you got correct for each type of graphic.

GRAPHIC SKILLS

Charts and Timelines (p. 34)	Maps (pp. 54, 114)	Graphs (p. 74)	Editorial Cartoons (p. 94)	Total for Graphics
14, 15	1, 2, 3, 12, 13	4, 5, 22	18, 19, 23, 24	___/14

Answers and Explanations

PROGRAM 11
THEMES IN U.S. HISTORY

Practice 1 (page 21)

1. **Asia**

2. **diseases**

3. **west**

4. **taxes**

5. **Declaration of Independence**

6. Answers will vary but should include any two of the following: Both European settlers and Native Americans enjoyed more agricultural variety; the Native American diet began to include such meat as beef, pork, lamb, and chicken; the European settlers added turkey to their diet; disease killed much of the Native American population; Native Americans began to hunt using horses.

Practice 2 (page 23)

1. **c**

2. **d**

3. **b**

4. **a**

5. Britain, Mexico, and Spain

6. Answers will vary. Some students may note that there was no geographic reason for the United States to stretch from the Atlantic coast to the Pacific coast. Others may note that Americans' determination to move west and to settle the land made Manifest Destiny inevitable.

7. The North became more industrialized, and more people worked in factories rather than on farms or in home industries. The invention of the cotton gin greatly affected the South. This machine made cleaning cotton easier, so cotton became a profitable crop to grow in the South. The increased growth of cotton led to an expansion of slavery because more workers were needed to plant and pick the cotton.

Practice 3 (page 25)

1. **no check mark** Abolitionists were people who wanted to end slavery.

2. **check mark** This statement is true.

3. **check mark** This statement is true.

4. **no check mark** The rebuilding of the South after the Civil War was known as Reconstruction.

5. Answers should include two of the following: The North's miles of railroad track enabled it to move troops and supplies farther and more quickly than the South could; the larger number of factories enabled the North to produce more munitions, uniforms, and other materials needed by the army and by civilians; the larger population of the North enabled it to have a larger army, as well as a larger workforce to staff the factories that produced war materials.

6. Answers can include any of the following: terrorism and harassment by Southern whites; Southern whites preventing them from voting; economic hardships; hardships based on denial of or lack of educational opportunities.

Practice 4 (page 27)

1. **b. transcontinental railroad**

2. **a. prejudice**

3. **c. personal computer**

4. **a. muckrakers**

5. **d. imperialism**

6. **b. Hawaii**

7. **d. isthmus**

8. The elevator safety brake made elevators safe and reliable enough for tall buildings to be practical. Without safe, reliable elevators, people could not easily reach the upper floors.

9. Answers will vary. Possible answers: the cable streetcar speeded travel within the city and allowed many people to commute longer distances to work; the telephone made communication instant and efficient; the light bulb provided a safer means of producing light; the electric power plant made electricity available to the whole populace; the automobile changed transportation and permitted greater and faster travel.

Practice 5 (page 29)

1. **Treaty of Versailles**

2. **Nineteenth Amendment**

3. **League of Nations**

4. **atomic bombs**

5. **c. It rose and fell and rose and fell.** The chart on page 28 shows that the unemployment rate rose from 1929 to 1933; it dropped from 1933 to 1937; then it rose again from 1937 to 1938; it fell again from 1938 to 1940, after World War II began.

6. **b. decreased it** When people are unemployed, they have less money to spend. Therefore, unemployment greatly decreased consumer spending. In fact, this caused the economy to spiral downward even further, deepening the depression.

Practice 6 (page 31)

1. **8** The Soviet Union collapsed. (1991)

2. **7** The United States and Communist China began full diplomatic relations. (1979)

3. **9** The World Trade Center and the Pentagon were attacked by terrorists. (2001)

4. **1** The Soviet Union took over the governments of Eastern European nations. (< 1948)

5. **4** The United States sent its first combat troops to Vietnam. (1965)

6. **3** The Korean War ended. (1953)

7. **6** Vietnam became a Communist nation. (1975)

8. **2** The United States stopped the Soviets from taking control of West Berlin. (1948)

9. **5** A U.S. astronaut landed on the moon. (1969)

10. The Soviet Union increased its military expenditures in the 1980s to match America's increased spending on weapons. This contributed to the economic and political collapse of the Soviet Union in 1991.

GED Thinking Skill Practice: Comprehension (page 33)

1. **(2) more rights for women** Abigail Adams asked that the Continental Congress "be more generous to them [the Ladies]" and "not put unlimited power into the hands of the Husbands." This implies that men had been stingy in sharing political power with women and that Abigail Adams wanted the delegates at the Congress to give women more political rights.

2. **(3) She was a smart and capable woman.** The paragraph explains that Abigail Adams ran the farm, took care of her children, read widely, and was concerned about the issues discussed at the Continental Congress. These details indicate that she was both smart and capable.

GED Graphic Skill Practice: Using Charts (page 35)

1. **(5) The Human Cost of World War II** This title is inclusive, indicating that the statistics include both military and civilian deaths and give the death toll for most of the countries in which loss of life was extremely high.

2. **(4) the Soviet Union** Read down the column that gives the death toll to find the largest number. Then read across to see which nation suffered this number of deaths. The Soviet Union suffered more than three times as many deaths as the nation with the next highest number of deaths, which was Germany.

GED Review: U.S. History (pages 36–37)

1. **(2) Four candidates competed in the election.** (Comprehension) The chart shows that the vote was divided among four different candidates. As the paragraph states, because none of the four candidates received a majority of the Electoral College votes, the House of Representatives voted, by state, for the President. This further complicated the election process.

2. **(4) Adams won because Clay got many House members to vote for Adams.** (Comprehension) To find the winner of the election, you need to look in the chart to see which candidate received the most votes in the House of Representatives. Adams received 13 votes, which was more than Jackson and Crawford and was a majority of the votes, as well. The paragraph indicates that Adams won because Henry Clay, who was Speaker of the House, lobbied for him.

3. **(4) Slaves lost what rights they had as their numbers increased.** (Comprehension) The paragraph explains that the first slaves to come to the Americas were often granted some basic rights and freedoms. As the slave population increased, the whites in power adopted slave codes; the slave codes deprived the slaves of their most basic rights.

4. **(3) The Struggle for Civil Rights** (Comprehension) This is the only title that is neither too broad nor too narrow in scope and relates to all of the events on the timeline.

5. **(4) Supreme Court decisions and acts of Congress** (Comprehension) The timeline indicates two ways that discriminatory laws were struck down: by Supreme Court rulings, as in *Brown* v. *Board of Education* in 1954 and by acts of Congress, as in the Civil Rights Act of 1964.

6. **(2) Women pilots took on noncombat duties during World War II.** (Comprehension) Most of the paragraph gives details about what the WASPs did in World War II.

7. **(2) between 1900 and 1950** (Comprehension) The graph shows that the greatest increase in life expectancy was made between 1900 and 1950, when life expectancy jumped from 47.3 years to 68.2 years.

PROGRAM 12
THEMES IN WORLD HISTORY

Practice 1 (page 41)
1. **d.** Sumer

2. **c.** Indus Valley

3. **b.** Egypt

4. **d.** Sumer

5. **a.** China

6. Answers will vary. Sample answer: The rich soil of river valleys encouraged people to settle there to farm. Surplus crops stimulated trade, which helped lead to the development of cities, advanced technologies, and record keeping.

Practice 2 (page 43)
1. **d** Roman Empire (44 B.C.)

2. **a** Babylonian Empire (2000 B.C.)

3. **f** Islamic Empire (750)

4. **g** Mali Empire (1235)

5. **h** Ottoman Empire (1361)

6. **c** Han Dynasty (202 B.C.)

7. **i** Aztec Empire (1430)

8. **e** Byzantine Empire (395)

9. **b** Greek Empire (336 B.C.)

10. Answers should include some of the following factors.

    Rise of empires: desire to gain control of more resources, such as land and labor; desire to control trade

    Success of empires: strong leadership of one or more emperors, good communication and transportation throughout the empire

    Fall of empires: weak leadership, rebellion of discontented groups, invasion by outsiders

Practice 3 (page 45)
1. **true**

2. **false** Feudalism is based on mutual obligation and loyalty between individuals; it generally arises in the absence of a strong central government.

3. **true**

4. **false** European nations formed through the consolidation of power of European kings, who all were hereditary monarchs.

5. **false** Nations first formed in Europe and only later formed in Asia, Africa, and the Americas.

6. **c. knight**

7. **a. king**

8. **e. has no corresponding term**

9. **b. noble**

Practice 4 (page 47)

1. **f**

2. **a**

3. **e**

4. **b**

5. **d**

6. **g**

7. **c**

8. Answers should include some of the following contrasts: The Chinese went on voyages to impress the world with their power and products and to command tribute payments. Renaissance Europeans, on the other hand, went on voyages of exploration to try to establish their own direct trade routes to Asia so that they could make money from this rich trade. When they reached the Americas, they began setting up colonies and claiming land and resources for Europeans.

   Both the Chinese and the Europeans were looking to increase their own wealth and influence.

Practice 5 (page 49)

1. **Britain**

2. **the United States**

3. **in western Africa**

4. **Italy**

5. **Portugal**

6. **Liberia, Ethiopia** (either order)

7. e, b, d, g, a, c, f

Practice 6 (page 51)

1. **Nuclear**

2. **medical**

3. **globalization**

4. **mass communication**

5. **airplane**

6. **Pacific Rim**

7. The workers are producing goods in Taiwan that will likely be sold in another country.

GED Thinking Skill Practice: Application (page 53)

(3) **The Hellenistic sculptors of Greece created realistic artwork that depicts ordinary people doing ordinary things.** Like Moche art, Hellenistic Greek sculpture was very realistic and showed people engaged in different activities from daily life. None of the other accomplishments is similar to any of the Moche accomplishments described in the paragraph.

GED Graphic Skill Practice: Using Maps (page 55)

1. **(1) north** (Comprehension) Use the map key to locate the symbol for the Nile's current. It is a blue arrow. Then find this arrow on the map. Using the compass rose, you can figure out that the arrow indicates that the Nile flows north.

2. **(3) sails, to allow boats to travel up the Nile using the prevailing winds** (Application) First locate Lower Egypt and Upper Egypt on the map. Notice that they both are centered on the Nile River valley. Notice also that while the river flows from south to north, the map shows that the prevailing winds blow from north to south. Therefore, the ancient Egyptians could go from Lower Egypt to Upper Egypt via the Nile River, hoisting a sail to help them travel upstream with the wind.

GED Review: World History (pages 56–57)

1. **(3) Jainism** (Application) The monk follows practices that would prevent him from harming insects and other small creatures. This practice goes along with the belief that it is important to avoid harming any living creature, which as the chart indicates, is a teaching of Jainism.

2. **(1) Hinduism** (Application) The chart indicates that Hinduism has ancient sacred texts; since Hinduism is the only religion that goes back more than 3,000 years, it follows that the 3,000-year-old texts the question refers to would be Hindu texts.

3. **(4) the Buddha** (Application) As the chart indicates, Buddhism teaches that the way to end suffering is the Middle Way. The quote uses the term "middle path," which is a strong clue that the quote is a Buddhist teaching and so was said by the founder of the religion, the Buddha.

4. **(2) Parsiism** (Comprehension) The chart indicates that Parsiism was founded in ancient Persia (where it was known as Zoroastrianism).

5. **(1) 100 years** (Comprehension) The paragraph says that the Vikings began attacking Europe in 800 and that in 911, their leader, Rollo, promised the French king he would end the attacks. By subtracting (911 – 800), you can see that the Viking attacks went on for about 100 years.

6. **(5) He had strong interests in both the arts and the sciences.** (Comprehension) The paragraph indicates that a Renaissance man combines interests in both art and science. The paragraph gives examples of da Vinci's accomplishments in both.

7. **(3) Baghdad** (Comprehension) The map shows that Baghdad was under Safavid control in 1629 but under Ottoman control by 1683. Therefore, you can infer that the Safavids and the Ottomans battled for control of the region that included Baghdad between 1629 and 1683 and that ultimately the Ottomans won.

8. **(4) the war between Sunni Iraq and Shiite Iran for control of the mouth of the Persian Gulf** (Application) The map shows that the land adjacent to the mouth of the Persian Gulf was the territory the Ottomans and the Safavids fought over in the 1600s. The Sunni in Iraq are the political successors of the Ottoman Sunni there; the Shiites in Iran are political successors of the Shiite Safavids.

9. **(4) America's Statue of Liberty** (Application) The information in the caption tells you that the Chinese protesters were demonstrating for more freedoms; from this, you can infer that their "Goddess of Democracy" represents freedom, liberty, and democracy, which are the same things that the Statue of Liberty represents. In addition, the "Goddess of Democracy" looks like the Statue of Liberty because, like the Statue of Liberty, the "Goddess of Democracy" also holds a torch.

PROGRAM 13 ECONOMICS

Practice 1 (page 61)

1. **choices**

2. **Land**

3. **Capital**

4. **entrepreneurship**

5. **labor**

6. **opportunity cost**

7. **scarce** or **limited** (either answer)

8. Answers will vary but might include giving up time with your family or income from a job.

9. They might have to give up less necessary goods, such as fashion items, luxury items, and other consumer products.

Practice 2 (page 63)

1. **true**

2. **true**

3. **false** They are willing to sell 60,000 jars at $4.

4. **false** The lower the price of grape jelly, the less grape jelly sellers are willing to supply.

5. Since the supply of grape jelly would increase, the price would drop.

Practice 3 (page 65)

1. **producer**

2. **consumer**

3. **producer**

4. **producer**

5. **consumer**

6. **consumer**

7. **producer**

8. **consumer**

9. 13.1 percent

10. Answers will vary. Your answer should compare your estimated spending in specific categories given on the graph with the percentages that the graph shows.

Practice 4 (page 67)

1. **false** Your money earns interest in a savings account.

2. **true**

3. **false** The interest on a CD is usually higher than the interest on a savings account.

4. **true**

5. **true**

6. 9.6%

7. 12.6%

8. 13.1%

9. Interest rates fell steadily during those three years.

Practice 5 (page 69)

1. **true**

2. **false** Part of the federal budget comes from borrowing money.

3. **false** The U.S. government is authorized to borrow money and, in fact, does borrow significant amounts of money.

4. **false** You may pay sales tax and/or an excise tax on the car.

5. **true**

6. **false** The government often spends more money than it takes in; this is called deficit spending.

7. **true**

8. about one-quarter, or 25 percent

9. $206.4 billion

10. about one-half, or 50 percent

Practice 6 (page 71)

1. **gross domestic product**

2. **consumer price index**

3. **unemployment rate**

4. **Japan**

5. **2000**

6. The consumer price index is closely related to daily life because people buy goods and services every day. If you are unemployed, another possible answer is the unemployment rate, which gives an indication of how many other people in the United States are seeking work.

GED Thinking Skill Practice: Analysis (page 73)

(4) High oil prices slow the U.S. economy. The large sheik represents high oil prices, and the worn-out slow moving horse represents the U.S. economy. The cartoon shows that high oil prices result in an economic slowdown.

GED Graphic Skill Practice: Understanding Graphs (page 75)

(1) one-half (Comprehension) The graph shows that 52 percent, or about one-half, of government revenue comes from individuals paying income taxes.

GED Review: Economics (pages 76–77)

1. **(5) wages, salaries, and social benefit payments**
    (Comprehension) According to the diagram, businesses pay households wages and salaries, and the government pays households social benefits, such as Social Security or unemployment compensation.

2. **(2) decreased spending on goods and services**
    (Analysis) When less money comes into households, the people that form these households have less to spend on goods and services.

3. **(1) Joe, a government worker who plans production output for the steel factories in his area** (Application) The fact that Joe is a government worker and that he is planning production output for factories gives a clue that Joe is working in a command economy, where output is determined by the central government, rather than by market forces. In the other options, the people are making economic decisions based on market forces or based on their own personal preferences.

4. **(4) They don't have money to hire extra help.** (Comprehension) In the first paragraph, the letter writer explains that because of budget cuts, the Tax Division can't hire many extra workers to help process returns.

5. **(3) delayed in processing** (Analysis) According to the letter, the returns that will be processed most quickly are the E-filed returns and the paper returns with 2D bar codes. You can conclude that handwritten returns will take longer to process. A smaller than usual staff will also add to the processing time. This means that handwritten returns are likely to take longer to process, so refunds with these returns are likely to be delayed.

6. **(2) wholesale and retail trade** (Comprehension) Look for the section of the graph that is about one-quarter, or 25 percent, of the whole graph. That section represents wholesale and retail trade.

7. **(5) There are six times as many service-sector jobs as construction jobs.** (Analysis) First compare the sizes of the two graph sections visually. Then divide the approximate percentage of services jobs by the approximate percentage of construction jobs: 36% ÷ 6% = 6. These results show that there are six times as many jobs in services as in construction.

PROGRAM 14
CIVICS AND GOVERNMENT

Practice 1 (page 81)

1. **executive**
2. **legislative**
3. **judicial**
4. **legislative**
5. **executive**
6. **judicial**
7. **executive**
8. **legislative**
9. **executive**
10. The framers of the Constitution were concerned that one branch or person would have too much power unless government powers were separated and delegated to different parts of the government.
11. Many Americans were concerned that President Roosevelt's lengthy term in office gave him too much power. Limiting the president to two terms was a way of preventing this type of concentration of presidential power from recurring.

Practice 2 (page 83)

1. **true**
2. **false** The Congress approves or disapproves the president's Supreme Court nominees.
3. **false** Powers are divided and balanced among the three branches.
4. **true**
5. **true**
6. **true**
7. **false** If national and state laws contradict each other, the Constitution stipulates that national law be followed.
8.

Federal Powers	Federal and State Powers	State Powers
• Coin money • Negotiate foreign treaties • Provide armed forces • Declare war	• Collect taxes; spend, and borrow money	• Regulate elections • Establish local governments • Exert powers not limited to federal government or prohibited to states

Practice 3 (page 85)

1. **b. Second Amendment**

2. **d. Fifth Amendment**

3. **d. Fifth Amendment**

4. **g. Eighth Amendment**

5. **a. First Amendment**

6. **c. Fourth Amendment**

7. **e. Sixth Amendment**

8. **a. First Amendment**

9. **f. Seventh Amendment**

10. **a. First Amendment**

11. **g. Eighth Amendment**

12. She is exercising her right not to testify against herself.

13. The First Amendment protects the right of free speech, including symbolic speech.

14. The Fourth Amendment protects against unreasonable searches; generally, this means that police officers must get and show a search warrant before they can search a person's home.

Practice 4 (page 87)

1. **property owners**

2. **Fifteenth Amendment**

3. **Nineteenth Amendment**

4. **Voting Rights Act**

5. **age 18 and over**

6. Grand juries meet in secret to protect the person under investigation. In cases where no charges are filed, the person can resume his or her life without bad publicity.

7. Answers will vary. Many defendants prefer a jury trial, because all of the jurors have to agree that the defendant is guilty for the defendant to be convicted. In a trial by judge, only one person needs to think the defendant is guilty for the defendant to be convicted.

8. Answers will vary. Common aspects of the experience include receiving a jury notice, checking in for the panel, waiting in a large room with other potential jurors, being called for a panel, answering questions to qualify for a trial jury, hearing a case, and reaching a verdict.

Practice 5 (page 89)

1. **true**

2. **true**

3. **false** Its goal is to nominate candidates and help them win elections. Once in office, the elected official keeps his or her party's support by promoting the government policies endorsed by the party.

4. **false** Members of a special-interest group share a common interest.

5. **true**

6. Answers will vary, but one way to redraw the cartoon to show a Republican victory would be to have the elephant's side of the seesaw touch the ground. This means the elephant (the Republican Party) controls the seesaw (Congress).

Practice 6 (page 91)

1. **b**

2. **c**

3. **a**

4. **d**

5. Being informed about the candidates and any referenda on the ballot will help ensure that voters make good voting decisions. It also allows them to vote efficiently, preventing congestion at the polls.

6. Answers will vary. Paper ballots, scannable ballots, and different types of voting machines are among the technologies in common use.

GED Thinking Skill Practice: Analysis (page 93)

1. **(3) A president may take any action to meet the nation's needs, if that action is legal.** This is a paraphrase of the second sentence of the paragraph. The other options do not correspond to the opinions given in this quote.

2. **(1) a strong president** This statement was actually made by Theodore Roosevelt. As the paragraph indicates, Roosevelt believed that the president should take the initiative when necessary to protect or further the welfare of the nation and not limit himself to powers listed in the Constitution. In this way, Roosevelt increased the power of the executive branch, concentrating political power in the office of the president.

GED Graphic Skill Practice: Understanding Editorial Cartoons (page 95)

1. **(2) You can't change things if you don't vote.** (Analysis) The woman is the central figure in the cartoon, and her opinion, as expressed on her T-shirt, is the strongest; the woman's T-shirt has a biting or sarcastic kind of humor. These are hints that the cartoonist holds the point of view that it's not smart to not vote.

2. **(4) They are part of the problem.** (Analysis) The man's shirt says he's not to blame for current political problems, but, in truth, he shares responsibility for these problems because he didn't vote against elected officials that instituted the problematic policies.

GED Review: Civics and Government (pages 96–97)

1. **(3) the legislature** (Comprehension) According to the Parliamentary Government section of the diagram, the legislature chooses the prime minister.

2. **(4) separation of powers** (Analysis) Voters elect the president and the legislature separately, so the legislature does not control the executive, as it does in a parliamentary government.

3. **(1) Segregating other facilities was legal.** (Analysis) Since the Court said that separate railway cars for the races were legal as long as the facilities were equal, many states concluded that it was legal to segregate other facilities in addition to railway cars.

4. **(2) plaintiff** (Application) By suing the store, Anna began the lawsuit. Therefore, according to the definition in the jury handbook, Anna is the plaintiff.

5. **(5) court reporter** (Application) Anna's job involved transcribing, or typing word-for-word, the proceedings of trials; therefore, according to the definition in the juror handbook, Anna is the court reporter.

6. **(5) a member of Congress** (Comprehension) The man on the left addresses the man on the right, who is holding a law, as "Congressman." And it is the job of Congress to pass the nation's laws.

7. **(4) Special-interest groups gain too much power over Congress through donations.** (Analysis) As indicated by the caption, this cartoon uses a pun on the word *bill* to get its humor and its point of view across. One meaning of the word *bill* is "a draft of legislation." Members of Congress vote on bills, which, if they receive a majority of votes, can be signed into laws by the president. However, the bill the special-interest lobbyist is holding is not a piece of legislation, but money. (*Bill* is another word for paper money.) The cartoonist is critical of the process depicted in the cartoon. Bribery—using money to gain political favors—is not only corrupt, it is also illegal. The cartoonist indicates that special-interest lobbyists and members of Congress are perverting the legislative process through bribery.

PROGRAM 15
GEOGRAPHY

Practice 1 (page 101)
1. **map**
2. **grid**
3. **latitude**
4. **longitude**
5. **equator**
6. **prime meridian**
7. **latitude; longitude** (either order)
8. d
9. a
10. c
11. b

Practice 2 (page 103)
1. **false** To make maps, which are two-dimensional, mapmakers use flat projections of three-dimensional maps (globes).
2. **true**
3. **true**
4. **true**
5. **false** Navigators used the Mercator projection, which shows true direction.
6. Greenland appears much larger on the Mercator projection. That is because the lines of longitude are as far apart at the poles as at the equator on a Mercator projection. Therefore, landmasses near the poles, such as Greenland, are "stretched out." On the Robinson projection, the lines of longitude get closer near the poles, so there is less distortion of landmass size everywhere, including near the poles.

Practice 3 (page 105)
1. **South America**
2. **the Pacific Islands**
3. **North America**
4. **Middle America**
5. North America (or Middle America)
6. Answers will vary. You should mention defining physical features of your region, such as coastlines, mountains, plains, forests, or deserts, and defining cultural features, such as ethnic backgrounds of large groups of people who live in the region.

Practice 4 (page 107)
1. **b**
2. **d**
3. **a**
4. **d**
5. **c**
6. Answers will vary. Make sure to include all of the regions from which your ancestors came.
7. Europe, because we share a common Western cultural and historic tradition, and Australia, because we share a common language and much of North America and Australia were colonized primarily by the British.
8. The landmasses of the Western Hemisphere are smaller than the landmasses of the Eastern Hemisphere. You can tell because more of the Western Hemisphere is covered by ocean than is the Eastern Hemisphere.

Practice 5 (page 109)

1. change it

2. adapt

3. 12; 100

4. air conditioning

5. wells; Colorado River

6. conservation, water use laws, reuse of wastewater (in any order)

7. The sprinkler is set so that water is hitting the pavement, which wastes water.

8. fine the resident for wasting water

9. Answers may include taking brief showers, turning off the water while brushing teeth or shaving, fixing leaking faucets, installing low-capacity toilet tanks, and watering sparingly and during off-peak hours.

10. Factors that make living in an arctic environment uncomfortable include extreme cold, lack of daylight in the winter, isolation, and lack of agricultural opportunities. Technologies that make living in an arctic environment more comfortable include warm clothing, heating indoor environments, artificial lighting, telephones and Internet access, having food shipped in, and building greenhouses for raising food in the summer.

Practice 6 (page 111)

1. c

2. d

3. a

4. b

5. c

6. Answers will vary. Your answer should describe land, livestock, water, mineral, and recreational resources in your area.

7. Answers will vary. Your answer should describe how one or more of the resources that you listed in question 6 contributes to the economy of your area.

GED Thinking Skill Practice: Evaluation (page 113)

(1) **Food production has outpaced population growth in industrial nations.** (Evaluation) Malthus predicted that the population would grow faster than the food supply. Instead, improvements in farming methods have caused the food supply to grow faster than the population in industrial nations like Great Britain and the United States. Thus, the widespread famines that Malthus predicted for Great Britain never occurred.

GED Graphic Skill Practice: Interpreting Maps (page 115)

1. (5) **San Miguel** (Comprehension) Locate the airport on the map. It is almost due west of Lima, just outside the limits of the metropolitan area. Then look for the city that is closest to the airport. That city is San Miguel, which is south and a little east of the airport.

2. (3) **3 miles** (Comprehension) To find distance on a map, locate the two points between which you need to know the distance. Place the edge of a piece of paper along the shortest distance between the two points, and mark off each point. Lay the paper with the marks along the scale of miles, which, on this map, is near the bottom of the map. Compare the distance between the marks to the scale of miles. In this case, the distance between La Victoria and Magdalena Nueva is about 3 miles.

GED Review: Geography (pages 116–117)

1. (1) **the central United States** (Comprehension) According to the map, the two largest wheat-growing regions are in the middle portion of the United States. One of these wheat-growing regions is in Minnesota, North Dakota, and South Dakota. The other is centered in Kansas and includes portions of some of the surrounding states.

2. (3) **Throughout Idaho, Montana, Nevada, and Utah, crops are irrigated.** (Evaluation) According to the map, the crops are irrigated throughout much of the American West. Irrigation involves watering crops. Irrigation in the West implies that the climate is dry enough to require such watering for crops grown there to thrive.

3. **(5) milk and cream** (Application) According to the map, the upper Midwest, including Wisconsin, is part of a region that includes many dairy farms. That means it's most likely that John will buy a dairy farm, which would produce milk and milk by-products, such as cream.

4. **(2) Subtropical crops grow in Florida.** (Evaluation) According to the map, Florida is in the Gulf subtropical crops region. Since warm weather is needed to grow subtropical crops, this is evidence that Florida has a warm climate.

5. **(1) African sleeping sickness did not spread into North Africa.** (Evaluation) According to the map, the Sahara stretches across North Africa. This desert is a geographic barrier to many types of animals, including the tsetse fly. If the tsetse fly had been able to move into the Sahara, cases of sleeping sickness would have appeared in North Africa. The map shows that this did not happen. Instead, the flies and disease spread to the south and east.

6. **(4) Asia and Africa** (Analysis) Look for the sections of the graph that are about the same size. Asia, with 13.3 percent of production, and Africa, with 13.8 percent of production, produced about the same amount of bauxite.

7. **(3) They go out on crimes from a home base.** (Analysis) Geographic profiling of serial criminals assumes that serial criminals usually return home after a crime. Then they venture out from home on the next crime. The computer program calculates the area the criminal is most likely to live in, based on the locations of the many crime scenes the serial criminal is suspected of being involved in.

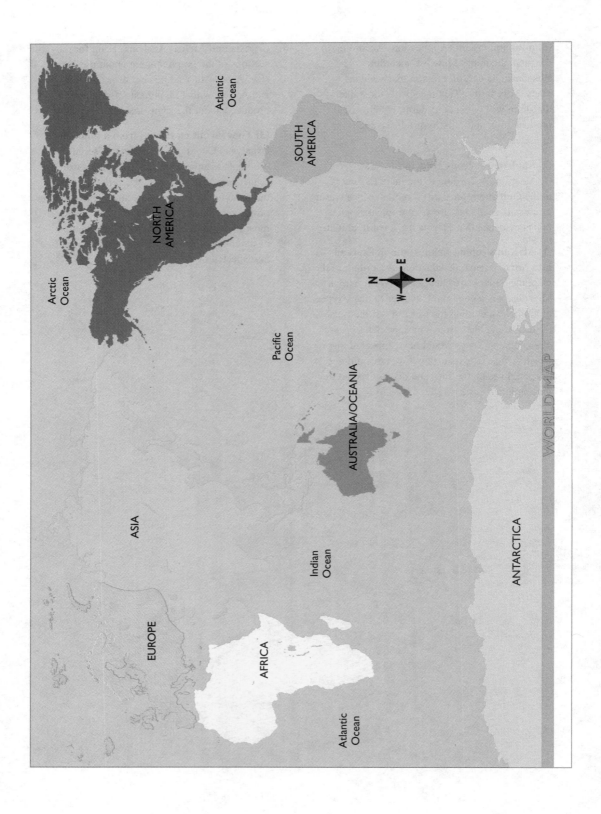

WORLD MAP

Arctic
Ocean

NORTH
AMERICA

Atlantic
Ocean

SOUTH
AMERICA

Pacific
Ocean

ASIA

EUROPE

AFRICA

Atlantic
Ocean

Indian
Ocean

AUSTRALIA/OCEANIA

ANTARCTICA

N
E
S
W

about 30,000 years ago

People first appear in the Americas; they give rise to the different groups of Native Americans

1600s

European settlers start colonies on the East Coast

1776

British North American colonies declare independence from Great Britain

1789

U.S. Constitution is ratified and becomes the law of the land

early 1800s

The United States expands and industrializes

Invention of the cotton gin leads to increased cotton output and, indirectly, to the growth of slavery in the South

1861–1865

Civil War fought and slavery abolished

1860–1890

New immigrants from Europe and Asia help build transcontinental railroads

Beginning in late 1800s

The United States expands its power and influence, following imperialist policies

1914–1918

World War I
(U.S. enters in 1917)

1920

Women gain the right to vote

1929–1941

Great Depression

1939–1945

World War II
(U.S. enters in 1941)

1945–1991

The Cold War between the United States and Soviet Union dominates world politics

1990s

Growth of technology increases communication between Americans and people throughout the world

2001

U.S. launches War on Terror

around 3500 B.C.

First civilization, Sumer, arises in Mesopotamia

around 3100 B.C.

Egyptian civilization arises along the Nile River

around 2500 B.C.

Civilization arises in Indus River valley

around 2000 B.C.

Civilization arises in China's river valleys

around 30 B.C.

Roman Empire arises

around 500

Middle Ages begin in Europe

around 700

Flowering of Islamic and Chinese cultures

around 1400

Voyages of exploration begin

around 1750

The Industrial Revolution begins in Great Britain

1800s

Europeans set up colonies in Africa and Asia

mid 1900s

Most European colonies in Africa and Asia gain independence

Advances in technology lead to a rapidly shrinking world and increased globalization

early 21st century

Globalization causes increased connections and conflicts among people of different cultures